Praise for Sacred Groves . . .

"Kathleen Davies' *Sacred Groves: Or, How a Cemetery Saved My Soul* is a singular odyssey, a spiritual journey that takes you through the maddening halls of academia and into the surprisingly healing graveyards of Ohio. With elegant prose, Davies crafts a beautiful memoir about diving into pain and coming out whole." - Marcy Dermansky, author of *The Red Car* and *Very Nice*

"In search of angels, Kathleen Davies describes her evolution from the contempt she experienced in the secular groves of academe to the exultation she found in the sacred groves of a cemetery. We need voices like hers to assess the current state of the humanities. Even though I don't remember making graduate students cry, I am proud to be a character in her book." - Susan Gubar, author most recently of *Late-Life Love*

"While experiencing 'death' in academia, Kathleen Davies finds herself inexplicably drawn to Victorian cemeteries. There she discovers the beauty of nature, images of female power, words that touch her heart, and at last, the buried child, herself. Her story of descent and return will open a way for others." - Carol P. Christ, author of *Goddess and God in the World* and *A Serpentine Path*

In *Sacred Groves*, Kathleen Davies turns a disappointing life event into a spiritual journey. An intriguing book by a creative writer and artist. - Maureen Murdock, author of *The Heroine's Journey: Woman's Quest for Wholeness*

Sacred Groves

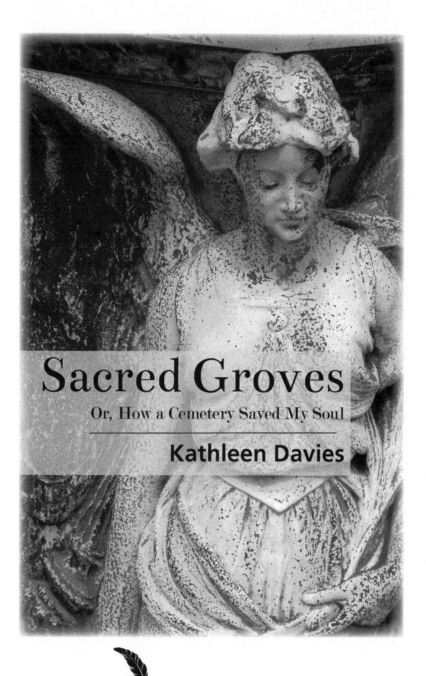

Sacred Groves

Or, How a Cemetery Saved My Soul

Kathleen Davies

Bink Books
Bedazzled Ink Publishing Company • Fairfield, California

978-1-945805-98-1 paperback

Cover Design
by

All photographs were taken by the author, except the following:
Portrait of the author in a cemetery: Macky Thompson.
Vintage hearse: A. E. E. Roberts Carriage Works, public domain.
Jaguar hearse from *Harold & Maude*: Replica by Ken Roberts, with permission.

Segments of this book have appeared in other publications:
"How a Cemetery Saved My Soul," a prize-winning essay in the 2017 Jung in the
Heartland competition, is available on the C. G. Jung Society of St. Louis website.
"Romancing the Stone" was published in *South Loop Review*.
"Stop Clock, Cover Mirror" (expanded version) was published in the anthology
*Guardians of Mediocrity: How Universities Use Tenure Denial to Thwart Change,
Creativity,* and *Intellectual Innovation* by Foiled Crown Press.
"Why I ♥ Cemeteries" was solicited by the Association for Gravestone Studies for
publication in *AGS Quarterly.*

Bink Books
a division of
Bedazzled Ink Publishing, LLC
Fairfield, California
http://www.bedazzledink.com

For Deb,
for her undying faith in me
and in this project

For Lynn,
for his undying love and support

&

For Others
trying to find their way home.

*May the Creator bless you
and help you find your way.*

Contents

Part II: Gathered Home

Invocations

May it be right to tell what I have heard,
May it be right, and fitting, by your will,
That I describe the deep world sunk in darkness
Under the earth.
~ Virgil, *The Aeneid*, Book VI

O Soul! fly back through all the grave-yards of thy Past . . . .
let us follow the heavy hearse that bore our old Dream
out past the white-horned Daylight of Love.
~ Adah Isaacs Menken, *Infelicia*

Call me Persephone, Queen of the Underworld.
Call me Demeter, searching for my lost child.

This is the story of a woman trying to find her way home.
This book is the wreath I hang on my door.

This Is Your Life

(An Introduction)

I REMEMBER THE moment I decided to write this book. It happened near dusk on a late summer evening. My dog, Mandy, and I were walking on a path in Woodlawn Cemetery, close to the border of trees marking the boundary between it and Gethsemane, when suddenly the light shifted and the headstones took on a different cast. I stopped walking to take in the sight, while Mandy, a black flat-coated retriever mix, sauntered off to sniff some delicacy that only a canine could appreciate. What I saw in place of the headstones were fragments of my life—moments, places and people I had known, parts of myself—all that I had left behind or buried for my career in academia.

And then it hit me: *Oh my God, my life is a cemetery.*

At first the idea struck me as hilarious. People who are drawn to cemeteries have an ironic sense of humor. But as with most jokes, there was truth in it, and Joke quickly shed his goofy jester garb for the priestly robes of Epiphany: My life *was* a cemetery.

Weeks before, I had spent weeks amassing documents for my tenure review. Articles, a three-hundred page manuscript, external reviews, course syllabi, peer evaluations, student evaluations and tables of numerical scores, summaries of this, that and the other—all and anything I could include to justify my existence for the past five years: hard, textual evidence of my *curriculum vitae*. The English Department on Main Campus required twelve copies of the articles and manuscript, so that the senior professoriate would have ample opportunity to deem whether I was worthy of joining their exclusive club, though I doubted many would actually bother to read my work. Many trees had sacrificed their lives for my tentative future, their pulp filling two large Xerox boxes that had to be wheeled up to the department on a hand truck. But my curriculum vitae and said pulpy evidence—my life on paper, as it were—seemed a poor substitute for the vitality I had lost in the effort to produce it. *Curriculum mortae* seemed more apt.

One afternoon during the peak of this frantic activity, I sat in front of my computer monitor wondering, *Do I even want this?* Naturally, I wanted job security for the rest of my life, not to mention benefits and a decent retirement. But I wasn't particularly looking forward to cranking out yet more textual evidence for further promotion. And what I most dreaded was getting stuck in Beantown, Ohio for the rest of my life, which would likely be the case were I to be granted tenure. Then I thought about all the time and effort invested, and fearing I might be jinxing myself with such thoughts, I told myself to snap out of it.

Soon after, I confessed my ambivalence to a colleague who had only recently survived the ordeal.

"Oh, everyone feels that way," she reassured me.

"Really?"

She nodded.

I had assumed I was the only one. But this woman—the one who followed all the rules and appeared to have one hundred percent dedication—told me that she, too, had dreaded getting tenure. Moreover, she was living proof that having misgivings didn't necessarily jinx one's chances. And yet somehow, this wasn't as reassuring as it should have been.

I'm going to write about this.

I said the words aloud, right there on the cemetery path, not caring whether anyone besides Mandy heard them. It was a moment of inspiration, and the words had all the weight of a vow that was long overdue. I had always wanted to write—not about what other people wrote, which was the lot of lit-critters, but about my own thoughts and experience. It was high time I got on with it. And so I promised myself that I would, whether I got tenure or not. I would write about how my life had become a cemetery.

Just as I was beginning to savor the rapture of pursuing a long deferred dream, inspiration struck again: *And I'm going to take photographs of the stones, so that readers can stroll through the cemetery with me. Black and white photos. Yes, that seems fitting.* Never mind that I had never taken a serious photograph in my life. I would ask my husband, Ben, to show me how to use his old Nikon. Take classes. Whatever was necessary.

I envisioned myself erecting monuments to the losses I'd suffered, each chapter a tombstone in the cemetery of my life. My life was a cemetery; why shouldn't my memoir be, too? The idea of a cemetery memoir was quirky, but that only made it even more appealing. And besides, with its memorials to the past, wasn't every memoir a cemetery? Or for that matter, wasn't every cemetery a memoir—a giant anthology of epitaphs and remembrances? This was more or less my line of thought when I had my Ralph Edwards moment and the subsequent epiphanies in Woodlawn Cemetery. But what I failed to realize that day was that, in choosing to write about the cemetery, I had invited the cemetery to be my Muse. And my Muse had other ideas.

For one thing, in the heat of inspiration, I had momentarily forgotten how I felt about the place itself. I was *ga-ga* for Woodlawn. From the beginning, I saw it as the only bright spot in Beantown. It was my sanctuary, my refuge not only from the hideous town but also from the idiocies of academia. It was my spiritual landscape—beautiful and numinous—and I felt at home there. Naturally, my Muse wanted me to write about all the good stuff she'd brought to me, so she began whispering in my ear, helping me to recognize the genius of the place. She kept insisting that I write a book about how the cemetery had saved my soul and called me to a more authentic destiny of being a creative writer as well as a scholar.

Admittedly, my Muse can be melodramatic. Victorian cemeteries are like that. But if "saving a soul" means helping me to keep what I loved and valued intact and to reconnect with an important part of myself, not to mention nurturing my sense of the sacred, then save my soul she did. She cultivated my soul, you might say, just as any good Victorian Garden Cemetery should do.

I KNOW ALL of this must sound odd. It *is* odd. But what I have discovered is that the soul works in odd ways. Renaissance magus Marsilio Ficino once wrote, "At different times the soul brings forth its variety of seeds more or less in profusion." My soul planted its seeds in cemeteries at precisely that point when I officially entered my profession. The first cemetery popped up within weeks after I completed my Ph.D.—I swear I'm not making this up—and then, after I moved to Beantown, I sought out Woodlawn as its replacement. It was as if cemeteries were meant to go hand in hand with my academic career, not only to mirror the sacrifices I was making but also to comfort me as I faced its trials. The day I decided to write about the cemetery's connection to my life, those seeds broke through the soil. After I was denied tenure—for that was the outcome, after all—and I began to visit other Victorian Garden Cemeteries and reflect upon the trajectory of my life, those seeds started to blossom.

So, yes, this odyssey of mine (or *odd*yssey, as I like to think of it) is peculiar to say the least, but I have also discovered that it is not altogether unusual, especially in its symbolic dimensions. According to Jungian psychologist Maureen Murdock, author of *The Heroine's Journey*, many contemporary women who have dedicated their lives to succeeding in male-dominant professions (academia being just one among many) have shared the alienation I experienced, reaching a point of feeling such profound disillusionment and loss that they must undergo a psychic "death" in order to reclaim themselves. In order to reconnect with those parts of themselves that were buried in the service of success, they figuratively "descend" into the darkness. Like the Greek goddess Demeter, who goes to the underworld in search of Persephone, her beloved daughter who was abducted by the god Hades, they must take a trip to the underworld of the subconscious to retrieve and reclaim the sacred feminine. During this process of descent, women may dream of dismemberment, death and tombs. They may dream of goddesses and cemeteries. Put in Jungian terms, my "underworld" was both real and imaginary. I didn't dream of cemeteries; I visited them on a regular basis. I didn't merely dream of goddesses; I came face to face with them in the cemetery statues I saw. It was as if my subconscious had been turned inside out. But just as Murdock describes, my journey through the cemetery also led to my own descent to exhume and reclaim something very personal and precious—a part of myself—I had buried in my own psyche.

It's not surprising that many women feel alienated in academia. In ways both blatant and subtle, it can be a hostile place for us. Between 1980 and 2000, the period that followed Title IX and coincides with the period when I was immersed in building a career in academia, the number of tenured males was increasing 30% faster than the number of tenured females, despite the influx of women at that time.[1]

In women's studies, one of my specialties, concrete concerns of real women took a back seat to theory couched in academese only insiders could understand. In her study *Coming of Age in Academe*, Jane Roland Martin reports that academic women are inherently pressured to identify against themselves and other women, a phenomenon that resonates with Murdock's observations. None of this to mention outright discrimination and just bad treatment such as I experienced after graduate school. Sadly, the status of women in academia does not appear to have improved much in the years since.[2]

Underneath the vocational crisis, my story is also about a spiritual journey that led to self-discovery. On that deeper and more personal level, my spiritual *odd*yssey connects to the multitude of others who are "in search of a lost soul," as Carl Jung once put it, and a spiritual home. Henry David Thoreau's observation that "the mass of men lead lives of quiet desperation and go to the grave with the song still in them" is more relevant than ever. And the usual paths for finding a spiritual home and soothing that desperation are, for many, no longer helpful. According to the Pew Research Center, increasing numbers of us—up to 37% of Americans—are turning away from traditional religion to declare ourselves "spiritual but not religious" and, like me, are open to having a spiritual experience wherever they happen to find it. In my case, the Sacred Groves of Academe, which hitherto I had found to be spiritually nurturing, ended up being replaced by the sacred groves of the local Victorian cemetery.

I wrote this book for these professional women and spiritual seekers and for anyone else seeking a more authentic way of being. And of course, I wrote the book for myself. Both living the journey and writing about it have been healing. I hope that reading it will be healing as well.

But back to the cemetery as a real place. My Muse is impatiently tugging at my shirt sleeve again, clearing her throat to get my attention so she can nudge me back on the path . . . .

PART I

WANDERING SPIRIT

Gate, Gateway:

1. Opening in a wall or fence; structure surrounding the opening, such as a monumental or fortified entrance, an arch; structure that can be swung, drawn or lowered to block entrance or passage.

2. signifying: point of transition; passage from one state or realm to another; to a space governed by different conditions, where a new state of consciousness may be attained; release from the cosmos, beyond the constraints of the human condition; a journey into the beyond.

3. symbolizing the threshold, marking limits or boundaries; separating the sacred place or sanctuary from the outer, profane world; from the known and unknown, the ordinary from the extraordinary. Often guarded by tutelary spirits who bar evil or unclean influence, permitting the good to be drawn in, protecting initiates from harm. Entrance and exit are to be clearly announced, lest supernatural powers be surprised.

4. signifying rites of passage (the initiate's passing through the "sacred gate"); initiation into the mysteries; the soul's entry into deeper wisdom.

5. marking the way to revelation, salvation; the "strait gate"; the way to darkness or light.

6. symbolizing not only entrances but also the unseen spaces beyond them, the secret power found there; marking entry into a realm of

GREAT SIGNIFICANCE: *e.g., cities, palaces and fortresses; temples,*
UNIVERSITIES *and* **CEMETERIES**; *Heaven or Hell.*

7. *the mouth of monster or goddess inviting entry; the maternal matrix,
vulva, holy yoni, signifying opportunity for rebirth, the beginning.*

8. *Ruled by Janus, 2-faced Roman God of the Gate—god of beginnings,
departures and returns. Youth faces the rising sun; Age, the setting. Janus
holds the key.*

ALL GATES ARE CONSIDERED SACRED IN THE BELIEF
THAT THE BEGINNING OF ANY UNDERTAKING IS DECISIVE
FOR COMPLETION.[3]

At the Gate

Still round the corner there may wait
a new road or a secret gate.
~ J. R. R. Tolkien

WHEN I WRITE about the gateway into Woodlawn, I find myself doodling its contours in the margin. First, the double archways—one for entrance, one for exit—with fleurs-de-lis gracing their peaks. Then, the rectangular surround, the notched parapet on top. In the space of the arches, the spears of the wrought iron gates. To the left, the pedestrian entrance, if I've left room in the confines of the margin. It seems important that I remember its shape, as if the shape itself holds power. As if the shape is the message. Gateways of grand design and scale make a statement. They issue both invitation and warning to those who would cross the threshold. This space you pass into is significant, they say. Do not enter lightly.

The first time I saw Woodlawn, I did not enter at all. I was in Beantown for my interview at the branch campus, and I hovered before the gate into the sacred grounds of the cemetery, just as I hovered before the gate into the Sacred Groves of Academe. The fact that I had sought out the cemetery was a measure of my desperation. I was worried that I might actually get the job and end up stranded in Beantown, Ohio for the rest of my life. I could imagine few fates worse than that—except maybe not getting a job at all, which, given the sucky state of the job market, was a very real possibility. (Forgive me for being a jerk about Beantown. Living as a grad student in Bloomington, Indiana had spoiled me for living anywhere else.)

I almost hadn't bothered to apply for the job. When I saw it listed in the *MLA Job Information List*, I actually shuddered. *Beantown? Where the hell is Beantown?* And what a name for a town. It seemed to reflect a yawning apathy, and indeed, as I'd later learn, back in 1831 the name had been pulled from a hat. *Beantown? Where the* hell *is Beantown? Eh, what harm could it do?*

Of course I landed an interview at the MLA convention, and *of course* that led to the next stage, an on-campus interview—the only serious nibble I got that year, as it turned out. And *of course* I gratefully accepted the invitation when the call came. "Oh yes, I'd be delighted," I said. *Oh yes, sooo delighted.* Since Beantown was only a few hours' drive from Bloomington, it was decided that I would come over from Indiana by car. It was January, the month of gates, named for that funny-looking little two-faced god.

THE EXIT RAMP off I-75 rolled down onto the strip mall on the east side of town. I spotted the Holiday Inn where they were putting me up. Oh, happy holiday! And something else caught my eye, something incongruous and quirky, sitting as it was in the midst of a strip mall—a bright yellow caboose, the town's tourist center.

"How quaint," I thought, managing for a moment to block out the fast food joints and other McBusinesses that engulfed this relic from yesteryear. It was nearly five. I'd have just enough time to run in, snag a map—just in case I'd need one—and get a taste of Beantown's history, before grabbing a bite and settling into my room for the evening.

I didn't know how very fitting an emissary that caboose was for representing Beantown. How, with what wry wit some clever soul must have lit upon this emblem. How, later, I'd look at that caboose and sneer as if it were a tasteless joke. Beantown is the town of trains. Railroad tracks crisscross the town at any old place they damn well please, and at all hours, trains stop on them to hang up traffic with gross disregard for the urgent comings and goings of Beantonians. One day, I'd be one of them, cursing before the tracks, late for a morning class. But for now, I was grasping for any semblance of charm I could find to hang my future on.

The next morning, I was to meet Tim O'Malley and Dick Millam, members of the English faculty, at the local Bob Evans Restaurant, not far from the Holiday Inn. The campus, a small branch of Big State University (a.k.a. B. S. U.), was located a few miles past the strip. It made sense that they would meet me at Bob's, so that we could easily move on to the campus after breakfast, but this meant that we would bypass Beantown completely. I wouldn't get to see it first-hand. That made me nervous.

At breakfast, Tim and Dick offered up no small portion of charm—not enough to hang my future on perhaps, but enough to assuage my anxieties for the time being. Tim liked to chat about movies. *Is there nothing else to do here?* Dick and I discovered we had parallel lives—first as undergrads at Ohio U., then as Ph.D.'s from Indiana U., and now, possibly, both of us in Beantown. We waxed nostalgic over Bloomington, indulged ourselves in it over pancakes and omelets. He and his wife, Susie, a librarian on the campus, often returned there, he said, all these years later. *Oh my god, he's been here twenty-five years, and he still misses Bloomington.* Neither said nary a word about Beantown. I would have to bring it up myself, somehow, and do it in such a way as not to betray concern.

"Tell me about Beantown!" I said brightly.

Tim, being departmental coordinator, fielded. This was serious.

"Well, let me put it this way . . ." He paused delicately, so that I could digest what he was about to tell me. "A couple of years ago, there was an article in *Newsweek* that described Beantown as 'gritty.' I'm afraid that description is . . . apt." When he came to the upshot, he looked me straight in the eye.

I was still trying to fathom what possibly could have motivated *Newsweek* to publish a story on Beantown, when the full force of Tim's words hit me.

"Uh, *gritty?*"

"*Yes.* Gritty." Hey, you had to appreciate the guy's candor.

Suspicions were confirmed, then. There was no denying it now. No more grasping at yellow cabooses in hopes that—maybe, just maybe—Beantown might be that secret great place after all. I had to see Gritville for myself before it was too late. I'd sneak away later between interviews and dinner for a private tour.

LATER THAT AFTERNOON I headed back down the highway past the strip mall, toward town. I was thinking of the campus and how very small a branch it was—only four buildings and two trailers for makeshift classrooms. "Locals call it 'the Twig,'" someone had told me, laughing. At least they had a sense of humor about it. What would it be like to teach in a trailer?

Cur-thump. Cur-thump. First set of tracks. The grit soon followed.

Beantown is one of those Rustbelt towns—that's what the article in *Newsweek* had been about. Postindustrial decline. In Beantown's heyday, around the turn of the century, her Captains of Industry prospered. Steam locomotives were built. Oil discovered—up through the ground had come a bubblin' crude. Business was booming—and then, it wasn't. After the Depression, Beantown never recovered. The AAA tour guide says that Beantown had planned for the bust, diversified, even triumphed. But it's a lie.

It was a gray day, with dirty slush lining the streets, a factor I tried to take into account. After all, winter doesn't bring out the best in any town. But winter wasn't enough to explain the jaundiced pallor, the morose demeanor of Beantown. People on the streets looked listless. Depression seemed to linger in the air like the globules of oil emitted from the BP Refinery in the south end of town. The rotary in the middle of Beantown was devised to center the town, give it heart or soul—and perhaps it did once. Now, however, it only served to add confusion, mock the disarray of mixed architectural styles, slow and congest traffic unnecessarily. In Beantown, my internal compass would always be askew. With North Street heading west, and West Street heading north, did I ever have a chance of getting it right? Beantown broke your heart. Or your spirit. Even if you had a job, there were too many who didn't or who struggled anyway. Economic distress aside, there was something else lacking; there was something *abysmal* about Beantown.

I passed burned out buildings with windows boarded up. Old Victorians, paint peeling, columns flayed. Chipped shingles on turrets. Rough, naked clapboards. This was one ugly, awful place. I felt sorry for the people who had to live in Beantown, but I didn't want to join them. Had a feeling I was going to anyway though.

It was then—after I'd seen the worst, or close to it—that I got out the map again and saw the large rectangle filled with clumpy little trees and neat little letters reading WOODLAWN CEMETERY. Preservation instincts urged, *Go there*, now, and off I went down Market Street, where the old Victorians stood their ground, impervious to the dilapidation a mere block or two away. I stopped at the intersection of Market and Woodlawn Avenue, where street becomes boulevard, hung a left, and drove toward the cemetery.

After several blocks, the gate came into view: the sturdy limestone structure, rather grand, with the large double archways and the smaller one for pedestrians, each blooming into a fleur-de-lis, the top notched like the battlement of an old fortress or castle. This was no ordinary cemetery but a lovely Victorian in Gothic Revival style, the likes of which I'd never seen before. My heart was racing. I couldn't wait to get a better look.

But then, as luck and lanes would have it, I got flustered. Appropriately, Woodlawn Avenue dead-ends with the cemetery, but a major thoroughfare runs perpendicular. *Which lane? Middle? Left? Right? Er, right—right?* The traffic whisked me along, and I found myself driving by Woodlawn, with the chance for only a glimpse. But what I saw through the black wrought iron fence marking the circumference made me gasp. The cemetery was filled with trees—tall, stately trees, like an old-wood forest. Even in winter, Woodlawn looked magical. The bare branches of the trees were dusted with white. Snow covered the grounds and dormant inhabitants like a soft blanket over a voluptuous body. Built upon the Black Swamp, the rest of Beantown was flat and naked, whereas by some geologic miracle or human intervention, Woodlawn had the contour of rolling hills reminiscent of Southern Ohio and Indiana. It reminded me of home.

Thank god, oh thank god. I actually said the words aloud in the car—not that talking to myself is especially unusual. Thank *god* there is one spot of beauty in this *hellhole*. Thank *god* there is something here I can connect to, something I can *love*. Oh, thank god.

Why I didn't drive through the gate into Woodlawn after I turned around, I don't know. Had to get back, I guess, or saw all I needed to for now. But another quick look confirmed—*yes, thank god*—and then I made my way back through the gloom that was Beantown, hastening my little Oldsmobile back to the seclusion of my room at "the Inn" on the strip, and once safely secured in said room, mustered all the melodrama of a Victorian heroine and hurled myself across the bed for a good, old-fashioned sob.

I'D LIKE TO say that I was distraught over the future of my career, that I was consumed with questions like, How will I ever be able to do serious scholarship here? Or, Will I find the intellectual stimulation I require? But that was not the case. My distress was brought on by more human concerns. I knew I was going to lose my boyfriend, Ray. Suddenly I understood this with appalling clarity. He'd never move to Beantown with me. He needed to be in a "hippie town," he'd told me, and I had seen—oh boy, had I ever—that Beantown was anything but that. And me? I thought that's what I needed, too—a big-hearted college town with a bohemian atmosphere; a haven for progressive folk; a town with coffee houses and delis and theaters that show indie films; and my hippie boyfriend to enjoy it all with me.

As graduate students, many of us expected to end up with positions on par with our professors—at big research institutions, in cool towns like Bloomington. Or if not quite on par, fairly close to it. Rarely were we disabused of this notion. On the contrary, our ambition was encouraged, and to hint that disappointment lay ahead must have seemed unnecessarily cruel to our mentors. But the pecking order in Academia all but ensured that disappointment. Rarely does one get a job at a school as "good" as, much less "better" than, one's alma mater, let alone in an appealing location. As for Ray, there were many reasons why he wouldn't be likely to move to Beantown with me, not the least of which his predilection for evading commitment in every aspect of his life. Even if Beantown had been a suitable place for him, odds were, within six months he would've taken off for the road.

On both fronts, professional and private, I was experiencing a Reality Check. It shocked me and shook me to the core. It kicked me in the ass. In a flash, I could see my grim and lonely future. Tragic sobbing turned into unladylike ranting—*I'm gonna die here, I know it. I'm gonna fuckin' die here!*—and then reverted once again to sobbing. For a while, I lay on the bed wallowing in romantic woe and abject disappointment, staring at the muted pastoral scene that passed for artwork on the motel room wall—a cornfield in mauves and purples, with a streak of turquoise thrown in to match the drapes and bedspread. Then I got up to splash some cold water on my eyes and prepare to meet my prospective colleagues for dinner.

A BRANCH CAMPUS wasn't exactly the ideal set up for a brilliant career. But even I had to concede that we were a good fit, the Twig and I. My fields of specialization lined up precisely with the department's needs, and coming from a small town in Ohio myself, I was a good match for the students there. In only a day and a half, I had grown fond of my future colleagues. Tim was charming and sardonic and—owing in part to his winsome expression and his diminutive stature (sorry, Tim)—terribly cute. With Dick, I had the bond of shared experience and an interest in Willa Cather. I instantly clicked with Obie Achebe, a Nigerian who taught African literature (I'm "Obi-Wan Kenobi!" he said by way of introduction, to put Americans at ease), and with Herb McDougle, who was hilarious and close in age. Ken Schmidt, the most prominent scholar of the bunch having published three books, seemed cold and distant, but I was determined to reserve judgment.

And then, there was Nan Arnold, the only woman in the department and the one who had told me the Twig joke. In Nan, I found a kindred spirit. She was, among other things, a poet and loquacious in the extreme. Tiny (she couldn't have weighed more than fifty pounds), she sat in a wheelchair, her body stiff and twisted with deformities (a severe case of rheumatic fever had stunted her growth and devolved into rheumatoid arthritis, I'd later learn), chattering away, every few minutes pushing her oversized glasses back up her nose with her cane. A quirky character, much like me.

I knew I'd be lucky to get a job at all, but especially lucky to get to work with these good people. And given my attachment to place, I'd no doubt make peace with Beantown, eventually. Years later, I'd actually miss the place.

Weeks passed without word. Then one night, Nan appeared to me in a dream. Her image was projected over a huge television screen, teleconference style. She was perched in her wheelchair, chatting away in her animated style, explaining something very important to me, thumping her cane in emphasis. When I woke the next morning, I couldn't remember a word she had said, but I knew I'd gotten the job. A few hours later, Hyacinth Beldon, the campus dean, called to make me the offer.

"How much time do I have to decide?" I asked her.

"Two weeks. But of course, we'd appreciate hearing from you as soon as you know."

I could've accepted her offer right then. It wasn't as if I had much choice. I was stalling. There was comfort in delay.

The psychic teleconference with Nan put the seal of fate on the matter. And probably it was fate that I got the position at the Twig and moved to Northwestern Ohio. The move would prove to be a virtual gateway into experience. In the years to come, I would learn a lot about a lot of things—about teaching and about myself, about the politics of scholarship and the grim goings-on in Academe, even about love and marriage.

I have come to see that January as a double gateway—much like the gate into Woodlawn—a double initiation, one into the realm of the profane and the other into the sacred. With the move to Beantown, I was at the gate of a new life that would sometimes seem to be the death of me. And through the gate at Woodlawn, I had glimpsed a cemetery that would revive me and usher me into sacred and spiritual initiation. Like great sibylline mouths of stone, the arches had whispered, *Come, enter these sacred grounds. Those who cross this threshold will never be the same yet more themselves.*

Garden of Souls

Cemeteries are gardens of the soul.
They fertilize not only the souls of the dead,
but also the souls of the living.
They feed the spiritual imagination.
They take us back to the acorn of ourselves,
that seed planted when we were born, or perhaps
before we were born, residing in the ether
of the other side.
And they help us bring that seed to bloom
and eventual ripening.

Last Rites

Gather ye rosebuds while ye may . . .
~ Robert Herrick

I WOULDN'T HAVE thought to look for Woodlawn had I not already been introduced to Rose Hill Cemetery back in Indiana. Mandy and I walked there regularly during what would be my last year in Bloomington. I had just defended my dissertation, so it had seemed appropriate to walk in a cemetery. Teetering on the threshold between the end of grad school and the official beginning of my career, I was in that liminal space of betwixt and between where all initiates stand, awaiting rite of passage. As Gail Sheehy explains, all such passages involve a "little death," followed by a rebirth into a new phase of identity. In fact, in certain tribal cultures, this metaphor of death and rebirth is enacted in the rite of passage adolescent boys go through for their initiation into manhood. After the boys endure a series of trials, the elders bury them up to their necks in sand or lay them in shallow graves lined with leaves before proclaiming them men. By that logic, defending a dissertation might well be occasion for a funeral. But for me there had been no funeral, just a cemetery down the street that showed up almost immediately after my defense. Close enough, I guess.

The only problem was, I wasn't ready to move on to the next stage. My rite of passage—my little death as a graduate student and subsequent rebirth as a Ph.D. of literature—was a miscarriage. Or maybe I just got stuck in the birth canal. Or hell, maybe it'd been a still birth. Certainly there was prematurity involved.

The year before I finished my degree, I'd taken a temporary replacement position at a conservative liberal arts college in Southern Indiana where I couldn't possibly have been treated worse by some simply because it was my job to take over the women's and minority lit courses. Miraculously, in the midst of fiasco, I'd managed to finish my dissertation, but when I returned to Bloomington, I was still traumatized from the bludgeoning I'd received.

My dissertation director had tried to put an encouraging spin on it. "The experience has made you stronger," she'd said. "I can tell." But I wasn't so sure. I felt shaky and depleted. I found myself weepy at the oddest moments. And I had trouble remembering words. I felt like a combat veteran with a case of PTSD who had managed to hold it together through the war okay, but once home safe, found himself falling apart. (And what had I learned from this experience? Mainly this: that there are some really nasty people lurking in the Sacred Groves of Academe, and those who are good—and tenured and soon-to-be-retired—are often wimps. Such is the banality of evil in academia.) And so, I just wanted to crawl back into the womb of my alma mater for a while. My old department at Indiana University had offered me an instructorship, making my return to Bloomington possible.

It was only two days after I defended my dissertation that I signed the lease to the apartment located within walking distance of Rose Hill—an apartment, by the way, that came far too easily so close to the beginning of a school year. The timing of it was so spooky I have come to wonder if the Fates hadn't arranged it. Given the trajectory my career would take—or indeed was already taking by this point—it wouldn't have been unreasonable to have seen it as a harbinger of doom. Of course, I didn't know about the cemetery's proximity until my friend Jane mentioned it.

"You live near Rose Hill," she said with all the bright-eyed ghoulishness of a seasoned taphophile.

"Rose Hill?" Didn't ring a bell, but could've been the PTSD kicking in.

"The cemetery. Don't you remember how I used to go there at night?"

Jane had a thing for cemeteries, especially Rose Hill. Exactly what she had done there at night I never knew. Something innocuous, I'm fairly certain, like writing in her journal or spreading tarot cards on a gravestone in patterns that might yield hints of the future or clarity for some present dilemma. Whatever it was, she had always made her treks to Rose Hill sound adventurous, romantic, and vaguely subversive. And who could resist that entirely?

"You might want to check it out," she added, arching an eyebrow to pique my curiosity.

I tried to picture myself sneaking into the cemetery at night, groping my way in the dark through a maze of tombstones with God only knew who or what unholy thing lurking behind them. Nope, I had no intention of taking a midnight stroll through a cemetery.

"Sounds like a good place to walk Mandy," I told her, silently adding *in the daytime*. I thought Rose Hill might provide a good turnaround in a long walk with the beautiful flattie mix I had adopted the summer before my hitch in Hell. I didn't think much more about it.

And then there was the skeleton glued to the living room window. I didn't think much about him either. When being shown the apartment by the landlord's son, I had recognized him as the trademark of the Grateful Dead, the one where the skeleton wears a wreath of red roses on his skull like a crown. I thought he added a nice hippie ambience to the place. Once I moved in, he became an emblem of nostalgia for an earlier time. One glance at the Dead skeleton and I was back in my first year in grad school when I would go over to Pat's place in the student ghetto across from the Indiana University campus to hang out after classes, drink a beer, and listen to some tunes. Pat was from Oakland, so the Dead was his sentimental favorite. He had been my friend then, later my boyfriend. I had spent the first half of grad school with him, and the Dead had played through the early years like a soundtrack of our lives. Now their famous emblem was dancing on my living room window. Everything is coming full circle, I remember thinking, ending as it had begun. Seemed fitting. But not scary. Or foreboding. Until I researched it some years later, I didn't even know that the Dead skeleton was a memento mori, the original woodcut swiped from Edward Fitzgerald's Victorian edition of *The Rubaiyat of Omar Khayyam*.

No, neither the cemetery nor the skeleton struck me as omens of the misfortune to come. It is only now, years later, that I'm even making the connection, and still, I see their appearance as more humorous than ominous. Sometimes I amuse myself by imagining a headline in a tabloid published for the entertainment of the gods: WOMAN FINISHES PHD; THRONGED BY MEMENTO MORI. I can almost hear the Twisted Sisters of Fate tittering with delight at their ingenuity while reading it over a breakfast of espresso and chocolate chip croissants, the Great Poet in the Sky nodding approval from on high.

WHEN MANDY AND I first walked through the gate into Rose Hill, I wondered why Jane was so attracted to the place. While there were a few interesting mausoleums and statues, they tended to be mixed in with the uninteresting monotony of modern headstones—plain, boxy rectangles of granite—which lessened their impact. Except for an attractive group of trees standing around the low stone wall near the front, the landscaping seemed haphazard and unplanned. There were no stunning vistas or picturesque views; rather, the back overlooked a construction company with a view of dump trucks and cement mixers. And Rose Hill wasn't much of a hill at all, but a slightly raised embankment supported on all sides by a wall of limestone cut from the local quarries. That and the meager metal arch marking the entrance were its only distinguishing features. Rose Hill would never capture my heart the way Woodlawn and other Victorian cemeteries of my future would. But it is said that people are drawn to the cemetery when they feel hemmed in by an existential crisis from which there appears to be no escape, and as the cemetery on which I projected my existential crisis, Rose Hill sufficed.

Was I really supposed to spend my life writing literary criticism, writing about literature for other people who wrote about literature, when what I'd always dreamed of was being a writer myself? What possible contribution could another dry tome hope to make to the world? Who cared about that? With teaching, you could make a difference in someone's life. But literary scholarship? Not likely.

Doubt crept in when I started writing my dissertation. The deeper into it I got, the deeper my doubt. But I didn't see that clearly then. Instead, I questioned myself. That seems to be my default position: something or someone bothers me, and I think something's wrong with *me*. And there was something about facing the daunting project of dissertating, as we called it, that dredged up every insecurity I'd ever had, going all the way back to childhood. *Do my parents really love me? Will I ever be good enough for them? And why* aren't *I good enough, dammit! And who the hell am I anyway?* My deep seated ambivalence toward academic scholarship was masquerading as an identity crisis, aggravated by the undermining issues raised by contemporary poststructuralist theory, which came down to a few nihilistic precepts: There is no hidden meaning to decipher in literary texts. No connection between authors and what they had written. And anything that smacks of transcendence (including metaphor, strangely enough) is considered suspect by default. The upshot: None of it really means a good goddamn. Hard to write an analysis of literature with that specter hanging over your shoulder.

I was so profoundly alienated by contemporary theory and its hold over scholars in my field that it hit me personally. It went against everything I believed in (I considered myself a "born again pagan" at the time), and my spiritual beliefs also informed my dissertation on women and nature. Feminist theologian Carol Christ has pointed out that the social and spiritual quests are at odds for many women, in large part because our society worships at the altar of worldly success, on which spirituality is sacrificed. I was aware of Christ's ideas, but thought I was immune because my work incorporated my spirituality. But my spirituality ended up being sacrificed nonetheless. Intellectualizing my topic had sucked the spirit right out of it and me. In fact, I remember the day when I first realized I had lost my religion. I was standing at the bedroom window of the house where I had lived most of my years in grad school, looking out at the deep pink Echinacea flowers in the garden, when suddenly it struck me: I felt empty inside. The spiritual connection I had always felt was gone. And I didn't know when or where it had gone, or how to get it back or what to replace it with. I didn't think I ever would. Not in a million years could I have predicted that Woodlawn Cemetery would one day reconnect me.

Maybe I had a case of arrested adolescence. Getting married at nineteen can do that to a person. About the time I had started my dissertation, a past lives astrologer told me I had an adolescent soul. "In this lifetime, your mission is to find work or service," she'd said. She thought being a professor was a good fit, though she noted that my inclination of wanting to combine spirit with intellect went beyond the bounds of Academe. Wasn't that the truth? Presumably, if I chose to accept the mission and succeeded, I would get to graduate to Adult Soulhood. I knew nothing about the levels of soulhood or whether I even believed in reincarnation, but like any good student, I wanted to graduate. Yet I was off to a lousy start, I couldn't help thinking as Mandy and I trudged through Rose Hill.

I remembered the astrologer saying I had been a scholar in the two most recent lives: in the late nineteenth century, a Moroccan Jew so devoted to his work that he swore off marriage and children; then in the U. S., an English professor who studied the Romantics. You'd think by now I'd be adept at playing the game. But that didn't seem to be the case. *Big help, guys! Thanks a lot.* Of course, she had also told me that the English prof had been a womanizer, albeit a "nice" one. Who knew what rotten karma he'd racked up for me.

Looking around at the gravestones, it also occurred to me that, if reincarnation really is how it works, a person could be walking in a cemetery and literally pass by his or her own grave without even knowing it.

Maybe disillusionment was the inevitable result of cultivating intellect. That's what I kept telling myself that fall. It had all been worth it, hadn't it? Whatever else might happen, I would always have my degree. The years spent writing my dissertation had been among the worst of my life, ranking right up there with my first marriage. (I had divorced before entering grad school.) But I was proud of what I had written—it wasn't bad. And now the worst was over, right?

I couldn't bring myself to ask the deepest questions, the ones at the crux of the existential crisis that had drawn me to the cemetery: *Is Academia right for me? Is that where I belong?* To entertain such questions was unthinkable. There was too much invested, too much at stake. So I buried them.

I HAD MET my hippie boyfriend, Ray, in early September, soon after moving back to Bloomington, while registering to vote. He was working a table the Green Party had set up. As he was looking over my driver's license, he noticed that we shared birthdays. This seemed reason enough to share dinner, too. A couple of months later, he moved into my apartment on Fourth Street.

Hippie boys were my sexual preference. In my mind, there was nothing as sexy as a man with long hair cascading down his back. In Ray's case, this consisted of a long, very thin ponytail snaking down from the back of one of the hats he always wore. "I'm a bald guy," he confessed sheepishly on that first date, then sporting a canvas safari-style jobby that he left on throughout the meal. But it didn't matter. Hair or no hair (or both, as the case may be), hippies have a sensuality that makes them fantastic lovers. Their radical defiance to the establishment only heightens the erotic charge. And the erotic charge between Ray and me was strong.

When I was young, I secretly wanted to be a hippie myself, but I had been born a few years too late. During the Summer of Love, Ray and I were only twelve. In the mid-seventies, when I was a college student, the spirit of the era was still very much alive on many campuses in the Midwest, but it was after my freshman year that I became a child bride, which sort of put the kibosh on the whole thing. I ended up moving back to my hometown, commuting forty-five miles to the nearest university, too far away to participate.

Ray reawakened those adolescent feelings in me. He was my alter ego, my last chance to experience what I had missed before going off to Career Land. He nurtured me and showered me with gifts and compliments. All this doting and sensuality was like a balm—just what I needed after my year away in hell, not to mention all those years before, locked away in the scholar's cell.

And if that weren't enough, there was the other strange thing that happened in Bloomington that year: The sixties made a comeback. Even the fashions had gone retro, with a re-blooming of colorful tie-dyed t-shirts and broomstick skirts. The new generation of college kids seemed eager to take on the causes of their elders. And the Peace and Justice Center had just opened in Bloomington, becoming a gathering place for hippies and lefties of all stripes. There, people met for strategy sessions, all-age dances on the weekends, and "open university" classes put on by local folk. I took the course on anarchy. But it wouldn't last. The Center closed soon after I left.

It was like living in a time warp, both amazing and intoxicating. I remember that year in smell—nuts and grains, sandalwood, and avocado oil soap (one of Ray's many gifts), a commingling of scents I can only describe as Essence of Bloomingfoods, the spicy fragrance you find in a health food store, which somehow encapsulated the spirit of Hippiedom and the years I'd lived in Bloomington.

"I'm soaking in honey," I wrote to friends in between job applications that October. *Beantown? Where the* hell *is Beantown?*

Ray made me feel loved as no one else had. Catch was, he couldn't commit to anything, and I already knew he needed to live in a "hippie town."

Soon after I got the job offer, I went walking in Rose Hill to ponder our future. Ray didn't want to be buried, nor did he want anyone to know when or how or where he had died. Did he prefer to dissolve into dust under a tree somewhere, in total anonymity, with the other little creatures in the forest? I was trying to wrap my mind around it, when I found myself drawn to an unusual headstone. At first, it seemed corny: a heart of granite, with *Precious Memories* carved in loopy script above a silhouette of a man and woman embracing in front of a sunset. With the outline of bell-bottoms and soft polyester shirts, they looked like something out of the seventies. But the couple they represented were Depression-era folks like my own parents and Ray's. The stone celebrated a long-standing marriage, apparently a happy, romantic one. And that was what got to me. Clarissa Pinkola Estés says to love means to stay, and this stone was a monument to staying. But how could you have that, or any kind of future, with someone who doesn't even want you to know when he dies?

"I don't have to take the offer in Beantown," I said after returning with Mandy from the cemetery.

"Oh, no. Don't do that." The response had been swift, the tone serious. And maybe a little panicky?

"But how will we be able to be together?"

"I take Fritz Perls' view. You go your way, I go mine, and if our paths should cross, then that'd be good."

His complacency left me speechless.

Then he continued with a declaration that haunts me still.

"I'm not sure I want to be here."

"What do you mean?"

"Here . . . now . . . in this life. I'm not sure I want to commit to life, so I don't see how I can commit to another person." There was a certain logic to it, a sense of responsibility even.

"Oh, you should never give up."

"You don't see what I see. To me, this is all one big horror show." He swung his arm wide, gesturing the panoramic sweep of environmental disaster. "I cry almost every day."

He was right, I hadn't seen it, at least not to the extent that he did. My horror show had more to do with social injustices which, in the face of total ecological destruction, "didn't matter," according to Ray. I found this single-mindedness exasperating; nevertheless, my heart went out to him.

"Do you know what happened the last time I decided to commit to life? I said, 'Yeah, okay, I'll do it!' And right after that, I was bitten by eight Recluse spiders. Eight! They're poisonous, you know. I keep telling you, God's a Republican." He failed to see that his survival was miraculous, proof that maybe God wasn't a Republican, after all.

"But since life can be difficult, wouldn't it be nice to have someone to go through it with?"

"You want a *marriage*," he said, emphasizing the word as if it were a scourge.

"Well, maybe something like that, someday," I admitted. For ten years after my divorce, I had disavowed ever marrying again, but in the past year or so I was rethinking my position.

I considered mentioning that Beantown offered all sorts of great opportunities for environmentalist monkey wrenching, what with the BP refinery being located there, but then I decided to let it go. I resigned myself to moving to Beantown alone.

IN MARCH, RAY finally took off for Arizona. He found it hard to leave, and there had been many false starts. But before we met, he had promised his parents he would follow them to Phoenix to help them build their retirement home, and by the time he moved into my apartment in October, he was already long overdue. We kept in touch, but I missed him terribly.

In June, I made the trip over to Beantown from Bloomington to find a place to live.

At the end of July, I was scheduled to move, but I was so distraught over leaving Bloomington, I had made little headway on the packing before Dad arrived to help. With the despondency of a slug, I was all but useless, and the poor guy ended up doing most of it himself. Quite a feat considering I had acquired fifty boxes' worth of books. When it was time to leave, he practically had to pry my fingernails out of the door frame.

Once the truck was packed, I waved goodbye to the little skeleton dancing on the living room window and quietly shut the door.

The Soul's Proper Territory

To live from the mind is to balance in uncertainty
on a high wire.
The soul is more grounded,
and indeed its proper territory
seems to be somewhere beneath the ground . . .
the level of ground where we plant our seeds
and bury our dead.
~ Thomas Moore, *Original Self*

Gates Ajar

O depth of mercy! Can it be
That gate was left ajar for me?
For me! For me!
Was left ajar for me!
~ Lydia O. Baxter

AS WE DROVE down Woodlawn Avenue, Mandy stuck her head out the window, panting, ears and tongue flapping in the wind with drooly excitement. Dogs have an affinity for cemeteries. It's as if they can smell the layers of bones molderinging in the earth. To Mandy's highly sensitive sniffer, the cemetery must have emitted a special perfume.

I was just as excited, though for less morbid reasons. I couldn't wait to drive through the gate for the first time. And there it was up ahead—just as I remembered it from the winter before—sitting solid and square at the end of Woodlawn Avenue, beckoning, *Come in, come in.* The gate at Woodlawn was grander than the simple wrought iron archway we'd grown accustomed to at Rose Hill, but perhaps for what I was about to face, I needed something grander. In less than a month, I would start my first full-fledged job as an English professor.

Back in June, I had discovered that real estate is a bargain in a town that scores 348 on the list of 500 Best Places to Live. This meant that rentals in Beantown were cheap, but unless I opted to live out of town, houses with modern amenities were hard to find. I ended up in a working class neighborhood with a homely two-bedroom that looked as if it hadn't been remodeled since the 1950s. There were remnants of that built-in mania of the era I'd seen in my parents' house: a breakfast nook in the kitchen with a counter and bookcase on the side; a planter built into the stairway; a desk in a stuffy alcove in the bedroom. The refrigerator was one of those plump GE models circa 1955, complete with light pink interior and half-moon swivel shelves as an added modern convenience. The bath was covered in tiles of shrill pink plastic (my parents' upstairs bath had pink tiles, too, but at least they were ceramic) and a hideously clashing wallpaper border of ducks. There was no shower. Not one of the rentals I had looked at had *that* modern convenience. At least it had a garage and a yard. Begrudgingly, I had signed the lease and paid the deposit. Once ensconced, however, I decided to embrace the homely quirks of my low-key fifties pad, and my native enthusiasm for new beginnings kicked in. It was soon after the move that I had taken out the map retrieved from the caboose months earlier, traced a route from Hazel Avenue to Woodlawn, and with trusty canine companion in tow, set out for the cemetery.

On some level, I knew that passing through the gate was significant. The grandiosity of the gate itself, along with the wrought iron fence surrounding the grounds, proclaims it. We tend to think that the cemetery gate and fence exist primarily to protect the cemetery and its inhabitants from intruders and vandals, but they also serve a deeper purpose: to distinguish the sacred from the profane. Making this distinction was deliberate on the part of the landscape architects who designed Victorian garden cemeteries like Woodlawn. They hoped that visitors could leave behind their worldly concerns when they entered the cemetery and find its sacred space ennobling or, short of that, comforting.

The image of the gate ajar symbolizes another kind of transition: from our world here on earth to the world beyond. Found on gravestones old and new, usually with the words THE GATE AJAR carved underneath, it suggests that the deceased has passed over to the other side—to heaven, that "better place" so often mentioned to comfort survivors. The image of heaven's gate has Biblical origins, but in the nineteenth century, it was made wildly popular by Elizabeth Stuart Phelps's 1868 novel *The Gate Ajar* and two sequels that followed. Remarkably, in the second of the series, *Beyond the Gate,* the feminist Phelps managed to turn heaven into a utopia or "better place" for women.[4]

When Mandy and I crossed the threshold of the cemetery gate, I could *feel* the shift we were making from the profane into the sacred. And I don't mean this abstractly as we do in jokes about crossing the state or county line. *Whoo Hoo! We just crossed the state line into Ohio. Could you feel it? Hahaha.* No, I mean quite literally that I could feel the transition in my body with a *zzzip!* shooting through my middle. It was a sensation I would feel every time we went through the cemetery gate. It signaled that Woodlawn was a sacred and numinous place, not unlike heaven.

WE HAD ENTERED the City of the Dead, but it sure looked lively. Since I had last seen Woodlawn, the trees had taken off their coats of winter white and put on lush green attire. By now it was August, and growth was reaching fruition. Yet beneath the trees were monuments to the dead and the dead themselves, reminding me of Emily Dickinson's observation that every summer "be The Entomber of itself." At the same time, the contradiction between the green profusion of the trees and the gravestones beneath them seemed to put a charge in the air. And I knew that this is what gave the place its power, and that it was the presence of death that made the place sacred. And I marveled at how lovely a place Woodlawn was—much more so than I had imagined it would be.

Just ahead, where the entrance road forked in opposite directions, we saw a statue of a female figure on a pedestal beneath a tree, her hands grazing its lower branches, her face and modest robes tinged with green, velvety moss. That she was female I had little doubt, though in her chaste ambiguity, she was nearly androgynous. Her face was placid and magnanimous, her arms extended as if to embrace all creation and welcome those who walked there. *Come, come.* Was she a religious icon? Not that I could tell. But there was an aura of divinity or holiness about her that suggested it. Seeing this statue gave me the impression of the cemetery as a feminine space. The statues I would next encounter only strengthened the impression. Except for the two reliefs of soldiers on the military monument, all the statues in Woodlawn were female figures.

I looked around to survey our options. The main road branched off into a number of serpentine paths, each tantalizing with possibility, and I found myself wanting to walk them all at once. But since that was impossible, I chose a path close to the front.

There we passed a pensive young woman in bronze, not quite life-size, wearing a Greek chiton, reading the inscription on the tablet next to her: EACH DEPARTED FRIEND IS A MAGNET THAT ATTRACTS US TO THE NEXT WORLD. The words reminded me of Ray and how I missed him and wished he were there with me. I stood staring at the deep red geraniums in one of the planters built into the monument, when Mandy spotted a couple of squirrels chasing each other up a nearby tree. *Oh goodie, playmates!* She lunged, but restrained by her leash, she could only go so far while they looked back smugly, figuratively thumbing their noses at her. How is it wild critters understand that a leashed dog is powerless to harm them?

The path continued between two tombs built into the hills on either side—*tumuli* in architectural lingo—and then ran into the Gros-Jean mausoleum, which squatted on a small island of plot. As we followed the path veering to the left, worldly concerns snuck up on me. In mere weeks, I would be teaching at the Twig, and frankly, I was nervous. I had started working on the syllabi—one for the pre-Civil War survey of American Lit, another for Brit Lit, which was scheduled to meet in one of the trailers—but my heart wasn't in it somehow. I was procrastinating.

Worn out, perhaps, by the move, culture shock, change itself. It didn't help that I kept trying to work at the desk in the stuffy little alcove of the bedroom I'd made my home office—quaint but unbearable. Better to work sitting on the couch downstairs, I decided.

I didn't feel like a professor. Or rather, I didn't fit the stereotype, in part because I was a woman. Simply deciding what sort of wardrobe I needed had been agonizing. I didn't feel comfortable cultivating an aura of omniscience and authority that would distance me from students. That just wasn't my style. If that was what it took to be a professor, I wasn't sure I wanted to become one. I'd already seen some of my grad school classmates—both male and female—go over to the dark side, becoming that haughty, ego-inflated caricature of professorial erudition that students loathed and I found repugnant.

Well then, I'll just be the un*professor*, I decided. Problem solved.

But would the students like me? Would my colleagues at the Twig? Not that it mattered all that much, since ultimately, the Twig would not have the final say about whether or not I'd be granted tenure in five years. No, my fate—that is, whether or not I'd granted a decent salary and benefits for the rest of my life—would ultimately be decided by strangers who resided over ninety miles away in the English Department of B.S.U., Ivory Tower Proper. *Gulp.*

The frenetic pace, intense pressure and sometimes ugly politics (remember my season in hell?) of the tenure track is comparable to the hazing frat boys put their pledges through. And I do mean fraternity; academia is far more fraternity than sorority. To be granted tenure, I was expected to write a publishable book-length manuscript of literary scholarship, on top of teaching a full load of lit courses, many for the first time (*read: extensive/exhausting preparation, not to mention endless paper grading*) and performing "service" (*read: mostly bullshit committee work designed to keep the machinery of university bureaucracy grinding*)— all on top of adjusting to living in this town to which the Fates had so carelessly flung me. And then there was the unspoken requirement: I also needed to be *liked*. Just as a pledge must win the affection of his prospective brothers to be deemed worthy of joining their exclusive club, so too must the junior faculty member garner the favor of his/her senior colleagues who, just like the frat boys, will one day make the fateful decision behind closed doors to either accept or black ball him/her.

Would I be able to do it all? And would it be good enough?
In the world of publish or perish, would I live or die?

Just as I was in the midst of pitching these existential questions to the universe, we came to a large mausoleum that addressed my fears:

LET NOT YOUR HEART BE TROUBLED
NEITHER LET IT BE AFRAID

The words were carved into the top of the monument's giant "headboard." They sounded Biblical (a quote from the gentle Jesus, I'd later find), but not so preachy as to be a turn off. And anyway I imagined them more as coming from those who selected the quote, family members of the deceased presumably, offered to any passerby who might need consolation. Life being what it is, they knew that, sooner or later, someone would need it. Yet I also imagined them as coming directly from the dead themselves—from Helen (1871-1950), Margaret (1873-1911), Stewart (1870-1910), Kirkpatrick (1874-1926), John (1877-1937), and John's wife, Palmyre (1880-1977), whose graves lay on the ground in the middle of the monument, covered with slabs of granite, each carved with a different symbol—cross, chalice, and dove—and inspiring quotation into the center; and their parents Calvin (1845-1898) and Catherine Brice (1840-1900), who were buried in the vault submerged in the hillside above them. The dead, who had perspective, who knew that matters such as whether or not someone got tenure didn't amount to much in the end. Who counseled one to face the matter bravely in the meantime, without worry of outcome. Whoever chose the inscription, I found it comforting and encouraging.

I looked closer at the monument itself, admiring its unusual structure, believed to be designed by Saint-Gaudens, I'd later discover. I took in the semi-circular walls of stone emerging from either side of the headboard and noticed that there were benches tucked inside for mourners or contemplators and that they were supported by lions' haunches, complete with clawed feet. Across the way, the cemetery's holding vault, where they stored bodies awaiting burial in winter back in the day, echoed the leonine motif, its top featuring a carving of a holly wreath flanked by a pair of snarling lions' heads.

Take heart, my friend. Have courage. Be lion-hearted.

Judgment Day is such a long way off, I thought. I can't worry about it constantly and stay sane. Why not allow myself time to adjust to my new situation, focus on teaching new courses, worry about books and scholarship later? Why not follow the wisdom offered?

LET NOT YOUR HEART BE TROUBLED
NEITHER LET IT BE AFRAID

I stood looking at the words, drinking in their nourishment, just as I would in the future every time we walked by the Brice monument.

Fortified, we went on our way.

MANDY TROTTED AHEAD of me as we headed toward the Grandfather Pines, as I christened the three tall specimens congregating up ahead. Nearby, on the hill where the path diverged yet again, there was a plain granite stone marked DAVIES. *Was it a foreshadowing of what lay ahead of me in Academia?* I laughed at first and then shuddered slightly.

The cemetery was so quiet, so tranquil. Not another soul was present that first day we walked there. Not even the din of traffic intruded. Woodlawn truly was an oasis in the midst of the noxious world surrounding it. A refuge from ugly ole Beantown and the Twig.

Further up the hill, at a distance, I caught sight of another woman in stone. This one held a wreath in one hand while the other propped up her head as if the weight of grief were too much to bear. Later, closer up, I would see that she looked stunned by loss. Later, I would identify with her. But that day, instead of walking up the hill to investigate, we opted for the path going under the stone bridge that served as an overpass.

A bridge. A bridge! *What could be more charming than a bridge in a cemetery?*

Was it meant to suggest a bridge from here to eternity? from earth to heaven? Or perhaps it symbolized the way of transcendence on the road to enlightenment. Something spiritual, I liked to think.

After passing under the bridge, the path split again, with one mausoleum sitting at the crux and another built into the same hill that supported the bridge. I noticed a large clay pot of coral impatiens in front of the door of the former; by December, it would be replaced by a Christmas wreath on the door. Nearby, on the right, we saw a wistful lady on a pedestal, leaning on an anchor, the Christian symbol of hope. BLACK designated the family name and someone—probably a descendent—had recently tied a pink satin ribbon around one of the pillars that supported her. I liked the gesture, both simple and elegant at once, tying past to present. The color would change with season, mood or whim. Today, memory is a pink satin ribbon; tomorrow, it may be red or black.

I took in more mausoleums. Several were grouped together near the cemetery's front and elsewhere, too. *The dead make good neighbors*, I couldn't help thinking.

And then, standing alone, straight ahead on the path was the most fantastic monument of all: an Egyptian Revival style mausoleum, complete with sphinxes. Reclining out in front of the structure, the two sphinxes guarded the inhabitants inside with stern solemnity. Above the bronze doors—turned a rich turquoise green with age—were long, flat vulture's wings flanking a horned disk of the sun, the emblems of the Goddess Isis, Protector of the Dead, Great Mother, and Knower of Life's Great Mysteries, similar to the carvings on the vestibule doors of her temple. Mandy found the sphinxes curious, and while she sniffed about,

I mounted the steps to peer through the spaces between the door's design of lotuses, symbol of death and rebirth also affiliated with Isis, rendered in the straight, spare lines of Art Deco. From the back, sun poured through stained glass of turquoise, green, and gold.

What a fabulous mausoleum. It made me see Beantonians a bit differently.

WE EXPLORED WOODLAWN for over an hour that first time, and we still hadn't seen it all. But I had seen enough to fall in love with the place and to find both heaven and haven there. From the moment we had driven through the gate, I felt I had entered the heavenly realm. And like Elizabeth Stuart Phelps's vision of heaven as a utopia for women, I found the cemetery to be a feminine place.

We were about to cross the bridge we had earlier walked beneath, when I suddenly felt overwhelmed by the magnificence of Woodlawn and my gratitude for it—so moved, in fact, that I blurted out my feelings without hesitation or self-consciousness to Mandy, myself and anyone else in earshot.

"Oh, this is such a beautiful place!"

And then, little louder than a whisper, I added, "I feel so at home here."

Years later, I'd recognize my quirky sentiment in a letter penned by Transcendentalist Mary Tyler Peabody in the autumn of 1835 to Miss Rawlings Pickman about visiting Boston's famous Mount Auburn

Cemetery. "How can I describe the feeling with which I looked again upon our gorgeous woods and heard the song of the wind in the pine groves?" she wrote. "I always feel as if I want to stay when I get there."[5] I, too, wanted to stay in the cemetery—or at least I found myself not wanting to leave.

Woodlawn had a powerful hold on me. It quieted me and instilled reverence. It soothed my alienation and satisfied my yearning for something deeper. It appealed to my melancholic and introspective nature and met my need for the sublime. And it was a sacred space, my spiritual landscape and sanctuary. All of which to say, it spoke to my soul. And as we exited back through the gate into the world on the other side, I knew that I needed to be there, walk there often. It was as if my life depended on it.

Wild-Flowers

I AM THINKING of the wildflowers in the back corner of Woodlawn, on the edge of
the bank below the railroad tracks—Queen Anne's Lace, Black-eyed Susan, lavender Phlox.

That first August, when I moved to Beantown, I used to pick small sprays of them and take them home. I'd put them in a small green vase made of clay, given to me by my oldest childhood friend, and set them on the antique washstand in my bedroom, the one made of walnut with the brown marble top. I had moved to Beantown alone, missed the town where I had lived before, the man I had there.

The flowers were an emblem of my desire, a wish for a lover, and most importantly, a pledge to myself that I wouldn't let my career crush my own untamed flowering.

Little Stone Houses

We paused before a house that seemed
A swelling of the ground;
The roof was scarcely visible
The cornice but a mound.
                    ~ Emily Dickinson

I SQUINT MY eyes, and mausos become cabins, headstones disappear. I picture myself with a basket looped over my arm, walking on the path to a neighbor's—Sunny's, or Ruthie's, or Joe's. I pause at their door, hand them a loaf of zucchini bread, chat about politics or the weather, compare notes on how the fish are biting at the pond this week. I admire their tomato plants, invite them to drop by my place later. Wind chimes tinkle in a nearby tree. Life is good at the Woodlawn Commune.

In the first months of walking in Woodlawn, I frequently indulged in the commune fantasy. I missed Ray, and he was often on my mind when I went walking there. We had talked about communes. In his travels across the country, he had searched for one he could call home, but he could never find one to his liking. "They talk about community," he'd scoff, "but there is no community." I had the sense that, even if he found the most idyllic community imaginable, Ray would not have been satisfied. What he longed for, he could never allow himself to have.

And me? What a joke. I knew I could never hack living in a commune.
I loathed physical labor and liked my privacy and creature comforts far
too much. I had only considered it for Ray's sake. But I was in search
of community, too, and doubted I'd ever find it in Beantown, much
less on the main campus over ninety miles away. And so, I turned the
cemetery into a commune, complete with hippie companions to keep
me company. *Oh yeah, that organic fertilizer is some good shit, man.
Nothing like a graveyard for fertile soil.* Silly. But I suppose it reflected my
own desire to feel that I belonged somewhere.

Feeling I didn't quite belong wasn't the fault of my colleagues at the
Twig. They were very welcoming. Back in June when I was looking for
a rental, Herb McDougle and his wife, Maria, had rescued me from the
Motel 6, inviting me to stay in their lovely old home on Kenilworth
Avenue, which coincidentally happened to be near Woodlawn. Nan
invited me to join an early fall gathering at Lucy Thompson's place,
a charming little house in the country not far from campus, made all
the more charming by the gardening skills of her friend, Bill McIntosh.
Both Lucy and Bill were newly retired. Smilin' Dick Millam (as Herb
called him) and his wife, Susie, were to host an English Department
brunch at their house in October. I enjoyed the company of all and
really couldn't have asked for more attention.

But still new to Beantown and recovering from the shock of having
been separated from my beloved Bloomington, I felt like a transplant
whose fragile roots had yet to take hold in foreign soil. What's worse, I
wasn't sure I wanted them to.

But I felt at home in Woodlawn, and the presence of mausoleums
only reinforced the impression of hominess. Mausoleums look like
little stone houses, after all, and when clustered together, as they are
at Woodlawn, they resemble neighborhoods. That's what inspired the
commune fantasy in the first place.

There are twenty-three private mausoleums in Woodlawn Cemetery,
arranged in about five neighborhoods. The architectural styles run from
Classic to modern, with effects ranging from frumpy to elegant and
materials from brick to granite. Not one even remotely resembles a
cabin, though on treks to other cemeteries, I would later find a few
small replicas of log cabins serving as headstones. Although I had fun
imagining it, the notion of living in a mausoleum doesn't bear much

scrutiny. One glimpse through the grille of a mausoleum door triggers claustrophobia. And of course, there are no modern conveniences such as electricity, with very rare exceptions. One being the Downing mausoleum in Mount Pleasant Cemetery, in Newark, New Jersey for the purpose of warming widow Parthenia Downing during winter visits with her dead husband, Paul. One might also risk being haunted by the other members of the household, who might well be pissed off at squatters.

Still, the impression of neighborhoods is irresistible. There rest the good Wemmers and Michaels and Lufkins. There resides King Ballinger and Ruby, one of his several wives. There, the McCauleys, Mehaffeys and Mitchell-Baxters; the Mackenzies, Diesels and Heralds; the Mosiers and Prather-Dalzells; the Collinses, Russells and Thompsons; the families of Wohlegemuth-Erlanger-Simmons. And there sits Chez Cheuvront, a squat chunk of stone with oversized columns, looking so French. Shrubs and flower urns, wreaths and ribbons adorn the premises. The scene looks like a page torn from a mortician's special issue of *Better Homes & Gardens* or an illustration for the *Gothic Martha Stewart* site.

Ivor Stravinsky once noted, "Architecture is inhabited sculpture." Does it matter if the inhabitants aren't living? I considered the mausos to be works of art. They satisfied my need for beauty and my love of the grand and ornate—the more extravagant the better. Like a case from Erik

Erikson's study on gender and space, I have always had a predilection for enclosed spaces—for houses and boxes—wombs and tombs?—and for old houses especially. (Phallic protrusions aren't half as appealing.) From houses to mausoleums wasn't much of a stretch.

One day I walked up the steps of the Mitchell-Baxter mausoleum to peer inside at the stained glass windows, two images of the three Graces, one on either side. In one window, the young women look happy and content, affectionately holding hands, one leaning her head on the central figure's shoulder; in the other, they are more serious and contemplative, one looking downward, the others upward toward the heavens. With the help of the sun shining through from the outside, their colors of pink, blue and green were bright and uplifting. The windows couldn't have been more beautiful or skillfully wrought, except perhaps by Louis Comfort Tiffany himself, who designed mausoleum windows for his wealthy clients. Several other mausoleums in Woodlawn had lovely windows, but only Mitchell-Baxter depicted human figures.

IN MY DAYDREAM converting cemetery into commune, mausos into cabins, I envisioned a classless society. But I was walking through the neighborhoods of Beantown's elite. At the same time, I was wondering how I'd fit into the elite institution of Academe, not so much at the Twig—where marginality seemed to bind us in a kind of congenial cynicism—as on the main campus, Ivory Tower proper. Did my colleagues there truly see me as one of them? Did I belong there?

My attempt to inhabit Academe was compounded by being stationed at the Twig. The situation was like living in the ghetto and hoping to make it with the social elite in the penthouses and mansions uptown. Or perhaps more fittingly, like living in a trailer park in Arkansas and hoping to mingle successfully with the sophisticates of New York City. Or in cemetery terms, like being buried in the Potter's Field with aspirations of being transferred to lie with the mauso-dwellers. Ain't gonna happen. Or at least it's highly unlikely. The people in both places—highbrow and low—aren't much different when you get down to it, but members of the upper class don't see it that way.

I had already had a taste of what to expect. A few weeks before, I had driven the ninety miles into the city to introduce myself at the first departmental faculty meeting of the new school year. Afterward, a few of the women came over to greet me.

"Why, you're one of us. You should be *here!*" exclaimed one, a fiction writer.

Onlookers appeared dubious.

"Here's my card," she said. "Give me a call the next time you're in town."

I was flattered. I especially liked that she was a creative writer. I didn't then know that creative writers tend to be marginalized themselves in English departments, that in the strange pecking order of post-World War Two Academe, creative writers fall somewhere in between literature scholars and composition specialists, theorists being at the top of the hierarchy. Nevertheless, I appreciated her openness to embracing me.

On the ride home, though, I reconsidered her words. What she had said smacked of those double-edged compliments one frequently hears, like "Wow, you look great! Did you lose weight?" or "Wow, you seem so much more sophisticated than your (hicky) family." Coming from a small town, I had an ear for condescension. However, in this case my "family"—my colleagues in Beantown—were far from unsophisticated. Her "compliment" spoke volumes about the low expectations Main Campus faculty held for their regional colleagues.

Then there was the departmental party, hosted by the chair of the English Department in his home on a Saturday night.

After navigating my way alone in the dark through a maze of residential streets, I finally arrived at Maury Singer's apartment. The place was packed with unfamiliar faces. (Having better things to do on a Saturday night, none of my colleagues from Beantown were there.) I tried to draw out a young man, untenured like myself, who was huddled over the hors d'oeuvres, but our professional chit-chat was lukewarm, and once it went cold, I made my way to a cluster of women, feminists mostly, a couple of whom I'd already met at the previous meeting.

First I spoke with Lydia Miserovsky, who was friendly enough, though she had been among those dubious onlookers at the faculty meeting.

"So you're from Indiana?" she asked. "Did you work with Susan Gubar?" Famous for co-authoring the groundbreaking study *The Madwoman in the Attic*, Gubar was known by every feminist critic.

"She was on my dissertation committee. Such a brilliant woman."

"Yes, she is. I took an NEH seminar with her several years ago."

Great, I thought, this is the stuff connections are made of. How ironic that my connection to Gubar would later end up biting me in the butt.

And then I met Patricia Smiley, so dubbed because in all the years I would encounter her in the future, I never ever *ever* saw her smile. She was young and attractive, if rather stiff, but it seemed she had a disability where smiling was concerned. "Oh well," I said to myself then, "maybe she's just not a smiling woman." Knowing that we women are expected to smile constantly as a sign of deference, I tried not to judge Smiley and her stony demeanor too harshly.

"Where are you from, and what is your specialty?" Smiley asked me.

"I'm from the Beantown Campus—" Before I could finish answering her, she abruptly cut me off.

"Well, that doesn't mean you don't have a specialty."

Did she really think that uttering such an incredibly patronizing remark was being supportive? By God, I think she did. As usual when I feel blindsided, my immediate response was an unintelligible stutter.

Had I read Jane Roland Martin's *Coming of Age in Academe*, I would have had a much better understanding of the experience. I would have seen that being a woman, even among women, was as significant a factor in my reception as being from the Twig. Martin points out that a woman trying to make a home in academia is like an immigrant trying to make a home in a foreign country. Here, the "Promised Land" is a patriarchal institution that views women's habits and customs, interests and values (many of which we were socialized to have) as "other," as "foreign." As in the society at large, women are seen as less competent than men. In subtle and not so subtle ways, women are made to feel that they do not belong. Many women initiates feel "uprooted" from their "Old World" and vaguely confused by the "New." Finding themselves in a somewhat hostile climate, they—like other immigrants—try to adapt to the "host" culture. "Better think and act like the natives," as Martin explains. Better conform, assimilate. And as frequently happened with those who immigrated to the U.S. in the nineteenth century, those who are best at assimilating often end up alienated from their own culture and from themselves, and some (like my archenemy on the campus in hell) even turn against their own less-assimilated group or newcomers. Some, as Mary Daly pointed out years ago, become "junior men." This is, as Martin says, the "high price of belonging."

By the time I arrived in Beantown, the number of women had increased dramatically in Academe. Thanks to the passage of Title IX in 1972, great strides had been made, as I well knew, having had only four women professors during all my years as an undergraduate. Yet despite all appearances, the state of affairs wasn't all that different from before. Furthermore, the superficial appearance of improvement can actually make the situation more confusing for the generations of women who followed the pioneers who broke through the barriers, especially since those pioneers were reluctant to share their experience or insights with their students. I loved my grad student professors, but they did not encourage us to break from the norm. Nor did they discuss the challenges that plagued them as "immigrants." Rumors were heard on occasion, but only one—a black woman, the most alienated of all, God bless her—ever spoke about her experience. She referred to her male colleagues as "the tweeds." Perhaps they had higher hopes for us and didn't want to diminish our enthusiasm with negativity. Perhaps they feared repercussions from bad mouthing their male colleagues or simply saw such personal disclosure as unprofessional. At any rate, when it came to my turn to immigrate, I was ill-prepared.

But I didn't understand that then. I didn't even know I was an immigrant.

I only knew that I was a stranger in a strange land.

WHETHER LIVING or dead, everyone must have their stations, it seems, and cemetery real estate reflects class distinctions. Only the wealthy can build mausoleums. Some people can't afford even the simplest marker. I felt guilty for liking the fancy mausoleums. As I strolled past one mauso after another, I could hear a little gnat buzzing in my ear, telling me it was politically incorrect to like the little stone houses. I had been trained to regard emblems of wealth and power with cynicism and suspicion, and rightly so.

According to the pamphlet of the Woodlawn Cemetery Association, those who built the mausoleums were Beantown's Captains of Industry—the oil barons, merchants, financiers, locomotive and real estate tycoons who rose to prominence in Beantown's heyday during the late nineteenth century into the 1920s. Wishing to create final resting places and accompanying monuments for themselves and their families, many were among the founders of Woodlawn itself. Unabashedly entitling the pamphlet *The Valley of the Kings*, author Anna Beehler alludes to the Valley of the Kings in Egypt where the pharaohs were entombed as a theme for the "great men" buried in Woodlawn. The pharaohs of Beantown.

With its sphinxes guarding the front, the Nathan L. Michael mausoleum—my favorite—must have inspired Miss Beehler's paean to these "kings" of Beantown, as did the miniature pyramid featuring the family crest on Job Taylor's plot mere yards away and the various obelisks of the cemetery. The Michael mausoleum seemed a study of contradiction and political incorrectness. It sat on the edge of what appears to be the Jewish section of Woodlawn. Was the Michael family Jewish? Did their nod to the pharaohs of ancient Egypt cause them discomfort? Did ancient history whisper in their conscience; or were their sphinxes, as befitting their species, forever silent? Maybe they weren't practicing Jews, or practicing anythings, and needed to draw upon symbols of the afterlife from myth instead of religion. Or maybe the Michael family simply fancied the style, which easily combined ancient with Art Deco, its angular shapes congruent with the sharp angles of Egyptian art. In 1917, when the mausoleum was built, its style was a carryover from the second Egyptian Revival, as the third, inspired by the unearthing of King Tut's tomb in 1922, was nearly on its way in. Because of the popularity of Egyptian imagery, it is not at all uncommon to see mausoleums in this style. I'd later discover that it was not uncommon for even synagogues to adopt this architectural style.

Only recently, seeing the newly revised edition of *The Valley of the Kings*, which is far more extensive and inclusive than the original, have I discovered that not only were the Michaels Jewish, they were also German immigrants, adding yet another parallel to this oddyssey of mine as a woman "immigrant" in Academe.[6] But as it was, I didn't care whether admiring the mausos was politically incorrect or bourgeois. I had a tacit agreement with myself that Woodlawn was a place where I didn't have to worry about taste or ideology. In such cases, I have found, the soul overlooks contradictions with ease, embracing contradiction for some larger synthetic meaning or purpose. What the soul wants cannot be reduced to ideology. Her needs supersede the human requirement for consistency. Like the Michael family, I needed to acknowledge what I loved, whether politically correct or not. More than to critique—which is what I did every minute in the rest of my waking life—I needed to embrace. Woodlawn was the place where I more or less allowed myself to do that.

I was a stranger in Beantown. I didn't know anything about the people behind the surnames carved above the mausoleum doors, nor did I care to. The mausoleums are public art, I decided, and that is a great gift, whatever else these people may have done. And besides, those little stone houses made me feel more at home.

"Welcome to the neighborhood," they seemed to say.

Ancient Familiars

OH, HOW I loved those sphinxes, ancient familiars of the dead, guarding the entrance of a mausoleum. They reminded me of dogs. Since ancient times, dogs have been deemed guardians and protectors at the gates of the afterlife and suitable escorts into the next world. Dogs have accompanied Celtic goddesses and healers, and have served as the familiar of the goddess Hekate and other women with supernatural powers.

And so was Mandy, my big black, feathery flattie, my familiar through the cemetery. I don't know whether she could see ghosts, but she was once spooked in a deserted ravine of a cemetery in Zanesville. As for being my protector, she was more likely to sidle up to a stranger and wag her tail than to scare anyone off. But she looked the part, and not only did I feel safer with her, I felt her symbolic significance.

On the first roll of film I ever shot in Woodlawn, I happened to capture Mandy posing with one of the sphinxes in front of the Michael mausoleum looking dead serious, so uncharacteristic of her I laugh whenever I see it. Mandy and the Sphinx: Ancient Familiars.

Cemeteries Here Are All the Rage

Let the place of graves be rural and beautiful.
Let it be under the free air and the cheerful light
of heaven.
Let trees be planted there. Let the opening year
invite to their branches the springing leaf and birds
of song, and when the leaves and birds are gone,
let the winds summon from their boughs sweet and
melancholy strains.
The Rev. E. P. Humphrey
Cave Hill Cemetery Dedicatory Address
Louisville, Kentucky, July 25, 1848

WE COULD HAVE gone to the Faurot Park instead. It, too, had trees. It, too, had rolling terrain. It even had a pond of its own. There was absolutely nothing wrong with Faurot. And considering myself a nature lover and something of an environmentalist, I thought that I should be able to make do with a regular park, that perhaps I lacked imagination or harbored a morbid streak that I should prefer walking in the cemetery. But compared to Woodlawn, Faurot Park seemed dull. There were no statues or mausoleums, no intricate network of paths to add texture or interest on a walk through the grounds. It did nothing for my imagination, and I certainly did not feel at home there. And most importantly, it did not seem sacred. And a sacred place was what I needed.

And so, despite occasional intentions to go to the park, I'd see Faurot to the left on Woodlawn Avenue, mutter to myself, "Yes, well, there it is," and just drive on by and through the gates of Woodlawn across the street instead. Head hanging out the window, panting with anticipation the moment the gate was in sight, Mandy indicated that she preferred Woodlawn, too, although preferring a landscape chock full of bones isn't surprising in a canine. And so we followed our instincts, be they of a different sort, and gave into Woodlawn's beckoning time and again.

Although I snubbed Faurot for being nothing but a park, what I found so appealing about Woodlawn was that it was so *like* one. And that was often the excuse I gave to people when I told them I liked walking there.

"It's basically a park," I'd say, hoping to assure them and myself that I wasn't weird or morbid. "People walk and jog there," I'd add for back up. "Some bicycle and rollerblade through the grounds, some even fish in the pond." This was not a fib; I had witnessed these uses of the cemetery many times.

More often than not, eyebrows were raised in reply, punctuated with a wan smile.

Of course, raised eyebrows were somewhat justified. Woodlawn isn't a park; it's a cemetery. *People are buried there.*

Yet I thought of Woodlawn as a super park. Or botanical garden. Or arboretum. Only with headstones. It was the headstones and statuary and other sepulchral art, not to mention the dead themselves, that gave it its sacred character and made it "super," but the place wouldn't have been half as super without the distinctive quality of its landscaping.

It was obvious that someone had put a lot of thought into creating it. The gate and entranceway, the layout and serpentine lines of the paths, the wide variety and careful placement of the trees, that wonderful old stone bridge, the pond in the back, most likely human made: all signs of aesthetic premeditation. Not only that, but mounted on the trunks of several of the trees found in the older section were name plates, specifying the trees' various cultivars. Black Walnut. Catalpa. Sugar Maple. White Oak. Bald Cypress. And many more. This is what reminded me of an arboretum.

YEARS LATER, I would discover that, modeled after Pére Lachaise of Paris and the estate gardens of England, the Victorian Garden Cemetery was the first multipurpose landscape. I'd learn that, like me, the Victorians gobbled up the new "rural" cemeteries, flocking to them in droves. Families visited the cemetery for regular outings, even picnics. It wasn't uncommon for the wealthy to treat guests to an after-dinner drive or stroll through Mount Auburn, the first American garden cemetery. Englishman Henry Arthur Bright, a friend of Nathaniel Hawthorne, marveled at the American trend: "Cemeteries here are all the 'rage.' People lounge in them and use them (as their tastes are inclined) for walking, making love, weeping, sentimentalizing, and everything in short."[7] Ministers, such as Pharcellus Church, emphasized that the beautiful landscape was also meant to encourage visitors to "commune with a higher world." Of course, that was part of Woodlawn's appeal to me, too.

After the founding of Mount Auburn in 1831 in Boston, every city and town wanted a rural cemetery of its own; it became a matter of civic pride. And so it was with the enterprising people of Beantown, Ohio who, somewhat belatedly in 1871, bought T. W. Dobbins's farm on the outskirts of town as the first step toward the founding of Woodlawn Cemetery.

The names of the new rural cemeteries—Woodlawn, Green Lawn, Green-Wood, Green Mount, Mount Auburn, Mount Pleasant, Swan Point, Laurel Hill, Elmwood, Oakwood, Forest Lawn—evoke the image of the garden. In fact, later, when I scouted other Victorian Garden Cemeteries, I could usually guess what type of cemetery I might be visiting by the name I saw on the map, though I quickly learned that "garden" in the name most likely indicates a contemporary memorial garden, whose dull and barren landscape interested me not at all.

Why was the garden cemetery was so popular? Because it filled a void for nineteenth-century Americans. Until mid-century, there were no public parks. As the first planned landscape open to the public, the garden cemetery served the function that parks would later satisfy. And here's an historical fact that I especially relish: the Victorian Garden Cemetery became a prototype for parks to come, directly inspiring the design for New York City's Central Park, whose architects, Frederick Law Olmsted and Calvert Vaux, had been prominent in the rural cemetery movement. And it's believable, isn't it? Just imagine Central Park with the graves and headstones . . . not all that different from a Victorian Garden Cemetery.

FOR ME PERSONALLY, Woodlawn was important because it served as a replacement for the "Sacred Groves" of traditional university campuses. Until I moved to Beantown, every university I had attended had sacred grove appeal. Indiana University, my graduate school alma mater with its green, wooded spaces and Gothic architecture clad in limestone, was the ultimate example. But the Twig was sorely lacking in sacred grove appeal. After all, a twig does not a grove make. And so, I was forced to find my sacred groves in Woodlawn Cemetery. Strangely, Woodlawn's Gothic gateway resembled the architecture of I.U. One day I'd discover that the limestone used to build it had actually come from Indiana quarries. I even heard a carillon ringing out from the cemetery office building.

Even though I had taken the expression "the Sacred Groves of Academe" to heart, I'd already had enough experience behind the scenes to know the university wasn't as "sacred" as it appeared to be. And besides, the cemetery was more poetic than any university campus. It was far "rounder," as Gaston Bachelard would put it. And Bachelard might have been talking about Woodlawn when he described the special landscape that would "concentrate the entire cosmos, uniting heaven and earth, within itself," the place where "everything seems to be in repose."

Please Follow These Rules

- A Speed Limit of 20 MPH within the grounds must be observed to insure the safety of visitors and workers.

- Pets, Bicycles, Joggers, Motorcycles, Motor Homes or Buses are not permitted in the Cemetery.

- Do Not Park on the Grass.

- No picnicking allowed.

- No one under 16 years of age will be permitted in the cemetery unless accompanied by a responsible adult.

- No Leaf Collecting or Commercial Photography is permitted without written permission.

- Ritualistic, ceremonial burning of various items is only permitted in appropriate metal containers.

- Balloons, toys, statues, ornaments and similar articles are inconsistent with the decor and maintenance on the grounds. They are not allowed and will be removed. Ceramic, plastic or concrete urns and plant stands of any kind are not allowed. No benches of any description will be allowed upon graves or lots without the permission of management.

The above rules are necessarily not complete and we ask all visitors to remember that, first and foremost, Cave Hill is a cemetery, not a public park. For many of our visitors a visit to Cave Hill is symbolic of their remembering loved ones with love and affection. Everyone's behavior should be guided accordingly.

Cave Hill Cemetery
701 Baxter Avenue
Louisville, KY 40204

Obelisks

All pillars or columns originally had a phallic significance,
and were therefore considered sacred.

~ Charles G. Berger, *Our Phallic Heritage*

OBELISK. TALL SHAFT of stone. Spear. Pillar. Phallus. The obelisk
seeks to dominate the cemetery, to tower over all the ladies and other
stone inhabitants of the necropolis. A commanding presence, it forces
the eye upward, toward the Almighty Father in the sky, to the top dog in
the patriarchal chain. An ancient figure, the obelisk, as old as patriarchy
itself.

I never much cared for obelisks. I suppose they add texture to the
cemetery landscape, but I always considered them something of an
eyesore, if I thought about them at all. For the most part, though, I
didn't pay them much attention. I tended to think of the cemetery as a
feminine space. I was in denial. I'm afraid this was a habit.

The first year at the Twig had gone off rather well, without incident.
My decision to focus on teaching and adjusting to my new surroundings
had helped. As had the congeniality of my colleagues, of whom I had
grown quite fond. Campus was a friendly place, a woman-friendly place,
seemingly. But in early summer, something happened that would trigger
a chain of events that would force me to wake up and see the landscape
more clearly.

One day, in my campus mailbox, I found a letter. It was from a male student I'd had that spring. He had performed brilliantly in the class and had even won the award for outstanding student in English. With his high forehead and beady eyes staring out through thick glasses, he was unusual looking—Nan joked that he looked like a serial killer—but the English faculty admired his intelligence. Upon learning he wrote poetry, I had encouraged him to share some with me, as a gesture of support. He had responded by bringing me a folder of about thirty poems of mediocre execution, too many to respond to adequately at the time. The contents of the letter seemed more likely to come from the mind of a serial killer than a fine student. Was it revenge for a less than enthusiastic response to the poems?

The first part was a chatty indulgence cloaking anti-feminist baiting. In the class, I had introduced the students to the metaphor in feminist literary theory of the pen as phallus; apparently, this student had decided to seize the metaphor as a call to arms. At this point, though, the tone was playful with references to the Cowboy Junkies and other pop culture figures. But then, the letter got nasty. "I'm thinking of writing a novel called 'City of Meat,'" it went. "Sex with a knife is the ultimate act of intercourse. And suicide is the ultimate act of masturbation." I was shocked. Not to mention repulsed. At the end, he noted that he'd been in a mental institution in Cincinnati for two years. Nan, who knew him far better than I, had wondered about a gap in his history; perhaps this explained it.

"Poor Nathan," I whispered to myself in the car on the way home across town. Was he really so troubled? As I considered the possibility of his derangement, I actually had tears in my eyes.

And then, it hit me. *Should I be afraid for my safety?* I was a woman living alone and my address was listed in the phone book for anyone to see. *Oh, he's such a little guy, I could probably take him*, I reassured myself. But who knew how much strength a madman could muster if driven by mindless rage? *Neh, still, I can't believe he'd attack me*. I was sure Nathan liked me and, according to Nan, was looking forward to taking my women's lit class in the fall. I probably didn't need to worry.

During this time, Ben and I were starting to see each other. I needed a second opinion. I showed him the letter.

"This is creepy," he said, after reading it. "You should be careful."

"You think?"

"Yes. Do you have a baseball bat?"

"No. Why?"

"Because you should have one on hand. Just in case. I'm going to bring you one."

I found the protective gesture endearing, not to mention comforting.

I decided that I'd better tell someone on campus—just in case. In case what? In case I were attacked or murdered? What purpose this would serve beyond justice was unclear to me, but I'd always heard that one should keep a paper trail in academia, so that's what I did. I told Hyacinth, the dean, and John Boyd, the faculty president. Not wanting this to hurt Nathan's reputation with the English faculty, I mentioned it to no one else, not even Nan. Doubtless an overly generous gesture.

I then wrote Nathan a letter of my own—a slap on the wrist ("How dare you write such garbage to me knowing it would offend me?") and an admonition to seek help and other intelligent peers ("Go to Mensa or something.") He responded without apology, "Well, you asked to see my work; I can't help it if you took it so seriously." This "work" had included no indication that it was fiction.

The incident and all that went with it had distracted me from my own work, but the summer passed with no violent attack from the bespectacled little misogynist, and I thought the incident was closed.

And it was, until the following spring—the time of year when the English faculty gathered together in the faculty lounge in Calvin Hall to decide who would win that year's student award. Rumor had it that the senior guys wanted Nathan—again.

Was this a battle worth fighting? I wondered.

I decided it was. That I couldn't live with myself if I let Nathan win that award without challenging it. Besides, he'd already won once. Surely, they'd understand.

Wrong.

"Are you *vetoing* us?" Schmidt asked, appalled at the gall of someone of lower rank.

"That never would've happened to *me*," O'Malley declared.

Gee, I wonder why, I thought to myself. *Could it be because you're a man?*

"What about character?"

"*Character?*" both men chimed in, eyebrows raised. My heart sunk. I should've known better. One simply didn't mention such old-fashioned words in the liberal milieu of a state university without the risk of being misunderstood. My colleagues knew I wasn't a conservative zealot ready to wield the sword of normalcy to serve some twisted agenda, didn't they? But I was dealing with what I call fundamentalist civil libertarians, for whom context is irrelevant. To them, freedom of speech applies only to the speaker, no matter how evil or creepy his ass may be.

Consequently, no one asked to see the letter Nathan had sent me. But I sensed they didn't want to see it, didn't want to face this dark side of Nathan.

"But he already won the award last year. Why not give someone else a chance?"

"But I hadn't had him yet," Schmidt countered. "He's such a fine student . . . the work he did this year in my class should be honored." Schmidt had been a Fulbright scholar in Germany the year before and felt he'd missed out.

"But what about my work?" I asked. "I found this incident distracting to say the least."

Nan nodded. The rest were silent.

"Well, if you must have Nathan, then I suppose I could compromise." Anticipating defeat, I had planned this strategy in advance.

"*Compromise?*" Schmidt said, dumfounded in disbelief. "That doesn't make any sense."

"Oh yes it does," O'Malley conceded, who frankly, looked relieved. He was not fond of confrontation. He explained that, as an administrator, he fully understood that this is what one does for the sake of conflict resolution.

"I propose that we split the award between Nathan and Maryclaire Stone." She was every bit as smart as Nathan, if not smarter and more original, not to mention a hell of a lot more mature, and all but Schmidt, who hadn't yet had her in class, knew it. Schmidt looked disappointed, but everyone agreed.

Ironically, I would later question whether Nathan deserved even the previous year's award when Herb's wife, Maria, told me that, in classes she shared with Nathan, he had passed off insights gleaned from his reading of literary scholars as his own.

And speaking of classes . . . Schmidt was scheduled to evaluate my teaching the very next morning. The evaluation wouldn't be as glowing as it might have been, but he seemed to have reigned in any bias he may have felt against me for besmirching his boy.

I KNOW IT wasn't shrewd, but I found it hard to let the incident go. The implications of it disturbed me. I sought out O'Malley.

"Tim, tell me . . . What if Nathan had actually raped me? Would you still have given him the award?"

"I-I-I don't know." Fundamentalist.

When I was in grad school at I.U., this very thing had happened. A male grad student got the award and then sometime later raped and held his wife, a fellow student in the program, hostage. But the outcome was different. When word got out, the department rescinded the award. I told Tim as much.

"And every woman I have told about Nathan understands the logic of that," I added.

"Hmm, well, I'll run it by Marian and see what she thinks." Marian was his wife, who taught at a nearby college. I never did find out the result of that conversation.

Next thing I knew, Hyacinth called a meeting of the entire English department.

"We are going to settle this matter," she said, officiously, "if I have to call in a professional arbitrator. And you will have to get very clear about the criteria for this award so this doesn't happen again."

And on it went. The table seemed split by gender; the women (except Hyacinth) seemed to get it, but the men either didn't get it or didn't speak up to lend support. I suspect the latter was the case with Herb McDougle, who tended to be rather mousy, not to mention untenured.

"'You didn't march in the streets, as some of us did, Kathy," the dean said. She always thought I was much younger than I was. "We fought for freedom. Censorship is a dangerous thing."

Since when is not giving an award censorship? I wondered. And I heartily doubted that anyone around that table had ever participated in a march or demonstration—except me. And an award is not a right, I could've told them, but an honor. But Jesus, what did I care anyway? I didn't even believe in awards.

"Well, I don't even know why we are here," I said. "I made my compromise. There's really nothing else to discuss."

Hyacinth looked surprised. And with a stern reminder that we still had to clarify the criteria for the award, we were dismissed.

Later, I suggested that, as a prerequisite to receiving the department's outstanding student award, a student had to abide by the student handbook. The others seemed to think this was reasonable. But when I tried to find a copy of the handbook to see what it said about inappropriate behavior toward instructors, I was told it was unavailable until summer.

When I finally got my hands on the new edition, I found that it said students were not allowed to threaten professors in any way, even if they hadn't intended to do so. I put copies of it, along with Nathan's letter (long overdue), in Ken and Tim's campus mailboxes.

When Ken poked his head in my office door soon thereafter, we briefly discussed the matter.

"Do you feel it's resolved now?" he asked.

"Yes, and no," I replied. "I'm disappointed that the campus doesn't seem to care about my safety."

"Really?"

"What else am I to think?" And they didn't care. I'd heard about a male student's aggression toward a female adjunct instructor after an evening class going without repercussion. And I knew firsthand about a woman student's rape on campus being kept quiet. When upon her request, I accompanied the student to talk to Hyacinth about it, the dean made it clear that she intended to take no action.

With that, the incident truly was closed, but I knew I had risked alienating Ken and Tim, who also happened to be the only senior English faculty at the Twig, and I'd have to somehow repair the damage and hope these two mighty obelisks did not seek revenge when I was up for tenure. (Nan's rank of assistant professor made her ineligible to vote on tenure cases; she had been granted tenure without promotion, a practice the department no longer sanctioned.)

And for the most part, I believe I was successful. In the following year, Ken stepped up his mentoring of me. As the other Americanist at the Twig, he took it upon himself to do so. He might not have been especially interested in women's lit—his specialty was sixties culture— but he deemed me a good writer, and he encouraged me to be more aggressive in sending out articles for publication. He introduced me to his buddy on Main Campus and also to my predecessor, whom I would ask to be an external reader of my book manuscript for the tenure review; invited Ben and me to dinner at his home; coached me on how to network.

As for the other, minor obelisk in the story, he is now the writer of a literary blog that elicits no comments about male authors and critics such as Norman Mailer, James Joyce, and Harold Bloom . . . defending the patriarchy one male author at a time.

A Grave Practice

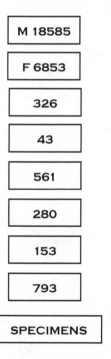

| M 18585 |
| F 6853 |
| 326 |
| 43 |
| 561 |
| 280 |
| 153 |
| 793 |

| SPECIMENS |

~ Grave Markers behind Psychiatric Hospitals [8] ~

Madwoman's Funeral

The maniac bellowed: she parted her shaggy locks from
her visage, and gazed wildly at her visitors. I recognized
well that purple face, those bloated features.

~ Charlotte Brontë, *Jane Eyre*

I WAS MAD as hell—pissed-off and crazy both. I always felt this
way when I had to face the idiocies of poststructuralist theory. The
idiocies *were* maddening. I felt like the lone voice of reason in the
loony bin. Chances were, I was not alone, but so few wanted to admit
their alienation, for to do so was tantamount to admitting you were
old-fashioned, unsophisticated, or just plain stupid. The theories were
couched in such impenetrable jargon that you always had this lingering
fear that perhaps you really weren't smart enough to grasp its intricacies.
I suspected it was designed to make most of us feel just this way.
Example: *discursive formations as coherent bodies in which power relations
and knowledge inhere.* See what I mean?

But here I was, having to face it all again. Sheer torture. I had to
figure out how to convert my doctoral dissertation on women and
nature into a publishable book that my senior colleagues down on Main
Campus would deem tenure-worthy. I feared that, like so many others,
they had gone pomo crazy and would expect my work to conform

to the postmodern mandate. Surrounding myself with books, the tall, unpruned trees of the neighborhood and my sidekick, Mandy, I stationed myself on the lounge chair on the patio to review just how dismal the state of affairs was for feminist literary critics like myself. The situation looked pretty bleak.

The problem was that, thanks to the hostile takeover of feminist criticism by postmodern theorists, my foundation had been yanked out from under me. Scholars build their work on the research of other scholars; that's the way the system works. It takes years of study to build this foundation; usually, your own beliefs are invested in it as well. To have it suddenly dismissed means starting from scratch, which is disheartening.

The building blocks of my foundation had appeared in the late seventies, just before I began graduate school. A particularly important one in literary studies was *The Madwoman in the Attic*, by Sandra M. Gilbert and Susan Gubar. They had argued that nineteenth-century women writers had created madwomen, such as the raving Bertha Rochester in Charlotte Brontë's *Jane Eyre* or some other alter ego, to covertly vent the rage and frustration that women were not then allowed to voice directly in a patriarchal society. *Madwoman,* as it was affectionately known, was a groundbreaking study. It was massive, sophisticated, and clever, yet accessible to nonacademic feminists.

Gilbert and Gubar's idea that women writers felt the "anxiety of authorship" strongly resonated for me since I had a good dose of that myself, and I was fascinated by the idea of reading women's novels as coded palimpsests with subversive subtexts. I saw some writers using nature in similar ways. This focus on women's literary strategies and traditions had been named "gynocriticism," and updating it with some important modifications that accounted for diversity, that was the school I claimed for my study of a women's pastoral tradition. I should've known better.

My other influences included the writings of contemporary ecological feminists Susan Griffin and Mary Daly. These were the madwomen come down from the attic. Their critiques of the patriarchal severing of humans from nature and their rallying cries for women's liberation empowered me both intellectually and personally. But by the time I embarked on my dissertation in the mid-eighties, they had been condemned. And oddly—or perhaps not so oddly—the condemnation against these pioneers had come from the pens of other feminists in the field. It wasn't that their shortcomings were merely criticized (which Daly especially deserved); they and their writings were dismissed. Marianne Hirsch witnessed this first-hand: "there is a certain generation of feminist theorists who have really gotten it from all sides . . . when you go to a conference and get attacked by other feminists—and I don't just mean criticized, I mean *trashed*—the whole tone and range of the project changes and *certain work gets disallowed.*" Although they continued to write books that corrected their oversights, their reputations had been virtually ruined in some circles, their work censured.

THE DEMISE OF *Madwoman* hit especially close to home. Susan Gubar had been my professor, after all. The inspiration from *Madwoman* had become inextricable from her. How I loved the woman's brilliance and wit—double entendre was her specialty—and her enthusiasm was beyond anything I'd ever seen. To Susan, experiencing intellectual excitement was like having good sex. When someone came up with a particularly clever idea in seminar, she'd moan a paroxysm of orgasmic delight (intoned in a strong Brooklyn accent), "*O-O-O-O!*"

In class, she was utterly charming, but one-on-one, Susan wasn't always so congenial. She was known to yell "Go away!" if a student happened to knock on her closed office door when she was busy. Brutally frank, she made every woman graduate student who wanted to work with her cry at some point. My turn came when I had sought her advice during the planning stages of my dissertation. Perhaps too inspired by the ambitious *Madwoman*, I had envisioned a massive survey, delineating a tradition of women's pastoral. "But you'd be *loony* to do that!" she said bluntly. Apt words from the co-author of *The Madwoman in the Attic*. Fortunately, I was able to stall my tears until after I left her office.

Her words reverberated in my mind for some time. *You'd be loony— loony—loony. . . .* Nevertheless, in the years to follow, whenever I got stuck in writing "the diss," I'd say to myself, "What would Susan do?" (*WWSD?*) and try to mastermind my way through it. Worked like a charm. For years, she popped up in my dreams as a guru. Her chain-smoking habit wasn't the best influence on me: *What would Susan do?* Light up! Wondering how many cigarettes she had smoked while co-drafting the seven-hundred-plus pages of *Madwoman*, I pictured a whole roomful of butts, from floor to ceiling. And apparently, I wasn't always the best influence on her; having just quit, she found herself smoking again when reading my dissertation the night before my defense. I don't want to know why; I like to think something in it excited her.

By now, I myself had quit smoking, though I wondered how long I'd be able to hold out. *What Would Susan Do?* was no longer a helpful question. What was *I* going to do?

AFTER RETRIEVING ANOTHER Coke from my vintage fridge in the kitchen, caffeine being my new best friend, I reviewed some of the charges leveled against *Madwoman*. Gilbert and Gubar's assumptions that novels reflect their authors' psyches and that a text may be interpreted at all were considered problematic and even "patriarchal." Indeed, that they even acknowledged that "texts" *have* authors and believed this to be relevant was deemed counter-revolutionary. *Mon Dieu! Mon Dieu!* Didn't they know the author was dead?

> For the patriarchal critic, the author is the source, origin
> and meaning of the text. If we are to undo this patriarchal
> practice of *authority*, we must take one step further and
> proclaim with Roland Barthes the death of the author . . .
> "Once the Author is removed, the claim to decipher a text
> becomes quite futile. To give a text an Author is to impose
> a limit on that text . . .[R]efusing to assign a 'secret,' . . .
> ultimate meaning . . . liberates what may be called an anti-
> theological activity . . . that is truly revolutionary."[9]

Confounding things even further, Gilbert and Gubar's focus on
women writers was seen as *essentialist*, since "the category of woman
writer is inevitably problematic itself."[10]

Essentialism was by now a favorite attack against the first generation
of feminist critics and theorists. Originally, it was a useful term for
the assumption that so-called feminine and masculine characteristics
were inborn. Because they are biologically female, girls and women are
inherently nurturing; whereas boys and men are "naturally" aggressive,
etc. etc. —an assumption long contested by modern feminists. But by
the time I found myself reviewing the state of feminist criticism on the
patio, I could see that the charge of essentialism was now being used so
sloppily and indiscriminately, it had nearly lost all meaning. Yet it was
an oh-so-powerful epithet: Just call a scholar's work *essentialist*, and you
could taint their reputation for life.

Like many others, Gilbert and Gubar were called out for using
the words *female/woman/women* generically when referring only to
white women (or rather in this case, white nineteenth-century English
women), thereby excluding women of color. Was that essentialism
exactly? Or a lack of consciousness? I thought the latter, for the most
part. I believed it was important that women of color had raised the
consciousness of us white women. But I had to wonder what the
alternative was. Did one really have to qualify "woman/women" or put
the terms in scare quotes every time they were used? Even when the
context was clear? *Really?*

If feminist critics who were exploring (some) women's shared
experience and literary strategies were being called essentialist, then
what was I supposed to do? Cut my losses, and gut my entire project?

That was exactly what Lydia Miserovski did, she would tell me a couple of years later: "After what happened to Gilbert and Gubar, I bagged literature and went into film studies." If I had been hired by a different sort of department—one where Gilbert and Gubar's work was still appreciated—this wouldn't have been an issue. After all, both critics had continued to build stellar careers, publishing numerous books and articles, receiving awards and much deserved recognition for their contributions. But by now I understood that the English Department at B.S.U. was interested in building their reputation, which meant they needed to be a "theory" department. Worrying about their criticism of my approach was bogging me down.

I had no one to turn to for advice. Nan wasn't in my field, nor was she an active scholar. As for feminist criticism, Schmidt wasn't an expert in my field either. My dissertation director had moved to Germany soon after I started it. Her co-director, who really hadn't been all that helpful, had died my first year in Beantown. It seemed unwise to reveal vulnerability to my feminist colleagues on the main campus. Nor did I feel comfortable consulting Gubar about the criticism of her approach. And besides, what advice could a sister gynocritic give?

How ironic that just as women were making inroads in academia and other fields, finally achieving more *author*ity of their own, some feminist critics wanted to discount authorship altogether or, like certain French theorists, argue that "the feminine" is that which cannot be written. Hmm. And how ironic, too, that with progress yet to be made, some feminists should "problematize" the term "women" (and with rancor, no less) and opt (as Tania Modelski so astutely put it) for feminism without women. Indeed, what *was* feminism without women?

Women kowtowing to a bunch of French philosopher dudes seemed anything but revolutionary, but this seemed to impress the men in charge. But then, maybe that was the point.

Sell outs.

This is what some women do in patriarchy: fight against each other. Vie for position at another woman's expense. And the men? No doubt some of them looked on, enjoying the "cat fight."

It struck me that this trend began in the 1980s when the backlash against the women's movement was rampant. So far, the 1990s weren't promising much better. The timing for my career really *sucked.*

BESIDES THE THEORETICAL issues, there was an additional complication for my scholarship.

My last year in Bloomington, soon after I defended my dissertation, Gubar stopped me in the hall with some bad news: Another scholar had already published a book on the same topic as mine. She happened to send it to Susan, who gave me her copy. "Yours is better," she said, "but on the surface the two look similar. You're going to want to think about how to distinguish yours from hers."

I thought long and hard about how to do that and also devise some pomo-proof strategies. I pondered not only that day on the patio but for the better part of a year, trying to decide if I could really pull it off. . . .

Maybe I could shift the focus from the women characters' relationship to nature (which would likely be condemned as essentialist) to how nature served to "authorize" women. I could retitle it *The Green Letter*. Oh, and maybe I should *expand* the dissertation! Not just write about twentieth-century fiction, but also the nineteenth century and poetry as well!

You'd be loony to do that . . . loony . . . loony . . . loony. . . .

And I was looney. Stark, raving mad to think I could execute that grandiose plan in the few years I had left.

And sadly, I never would find an adequate foundation for the project.

As for the fate of *Madwoman,* there were many who would continue to appreciate it, along with *No Man's* Land, the three-volume masterwork on a diverse range of twentieth-century American women authors that came later. And Susan herself would publish two works that grappled with what had happened to the field. Deciding feminist criticism was ill, not

dead as she originally wanted to argue, she would offer her diagnosis in a very rational, professional manner, even trying to see it in a positive way ultimately, as is her wont. "Yes, it was painful to be derided," she would write, "but I did not then and do not now want my personal discomfort to be used to discount what I believed and still believe about . . . the unproductive divisiveness in feminist scholarship."[11]

In 2008, Susan would be diagnosed with advanced ovarian cancer. She would write a memoir about it—of course!—and amidst the agony she would endure, would somehow continue to write, including a blog about coping with cancer for *The New York Times*. She would email updates to her former students, signed "Hugs, Susan," suggesting that the disease softened her, making her more openly affectionate to those even beyond her circle. And against all odds, she would survive for years to come. For her strength and persistence, I will always admire Susan Gubar.

Beloved Husband

Beloved Husband. Beloved Wife.
Spousal epitaphs warmed my heart.
Made me wish for a partner of my own.
Someone to love and be loved by.

Till Death Do Us Part

Come grow old with me;
The best is yet to be.
~ Robert Browning

BEN AND I stood before the altar clasping hands as we exchanged our vows.

"This is the happiest day of my life," he'd told me earlier that day. And I could tell it was true. He looked radiant.

"I pronounce you husband and wife," the minister said, putting her own hands over ours in blessing. "You may now kiss."

Putting his arms around me, Ben—a good head taller—bent down to kiss me, as I lifted my lips to meet his.

The small group of family and close friends, most from the Twig, applauded. Our best men congratulated us with hugs. (At the last minute, my maid of honor couldn't make it, so I asked a male friend from Bloomington to cover.) Then, after we walked down the aisle, everyone headed outside to form a reception line.

The venue was the Beantown United Methodist Church, a quaint country church just outside of town. I was raised Methodist, Ben Nazarene, and though neither of us considered ourselves religious, I wanted our ceremony to take place in a small church, surrounded by family and friends to witness and support our decision.

Outside it was a beautiful, sunny day, rare in late March. I glanced over at the angel statue in the churchyard, which I would one day photograph and frame for Nan as a goodbye gift. We chose spring break instead of summer for our wedding because that summer was critical for my career and I needed to focus exclusively on scholarship. This meant my parents had to make a special trip up from their winter home in Florida. My mother was none too pleased about that.

In the reception line, Dad gave me a chaste little kiss with tears in his eyes, which I sensed were more from disappointment than joy. In Dad's mind, Ben was not good husband material. That Mom felt that way was understood. She was the one who had always quipped, "You can fall in love with a doctor just as easily as with a poor man." But Dad tended to be more subtle—with tears in his eyes, teeth sucking sounds of disapproval and the like. In a way, they were right about Ben. Still a student at the Twig, he had few material resources to offer—so few, in fact, I was surprised that he proposed. He had just turned thirty two, and in a month, I'd turn forty. For now, I would be the breadwinner. My feminist friends reassured me this was all right and not to worry about others' judgments. And I had faith in Ben's abilities to secure a good job after he graduated. After all, he was very intelligent and an excellent student. Surely that suggested a promising future.

After hugs and handshaking, guests headed over to the reception dinner in Beantown, while our families returned with us to the sanctuary for pictures to be taken by my older brother and his eldest—both named Dan—an arrangement that came in handy when we took pictures with each family. For the pictures of us with my family—Mom and Dad, my brother and his wife, and their two daughters—Dad held my hand. With two grandparents, his parents, three siblings and their children, along with his cousin and his wife, Ben's family was nearly three times the size of mine.

"Hey, Kathy #3," his brother said smiling, "say cheese!"

I had just been inducted into the Kathy club. Both of Ben's sisters-in-laws were named Kathy, so in fun we were each designated by order: Kathy 1, Kathy 2, and me, Kathy 3. Later, when the middle brother, Keith, divorced his Kathy, I would get promoted to #2.

The church was decorated for Easter. On the wall behind us was a large purple wall hanging, embroidered with a bloody crown of thorns on a large white cross, along with the words "Once and for All" and bright red drops of blood spurting from the sides. Not exactly the best backdrop for wedding pictures, though my fundamentalist in-laws probably loved it. I always liked the symbolism of the resurrection, but the brutality of the crucifixion—the blood sacrifice—made me cringe. What, if anything, did the Easter symbolism mean for us and our marriage? Sacrifice or rebirth? Both, most likely, since both are part of marriage.

BEN AND I met when he was in my composition class two winters before. He was one of only two students (I couldn't believe the campus let that fly), so we had an unusually high amount of interaction in class, even more so since Ben was unusually engaged, while the other student was disinclined to participate much at all. That spring, after the class was over, we continued contact with his regular visits to my office for chats, not getting involved until that summer. Mandy took to Ben instantly, running out to his car to greet him when he arrived for his first visit. We kept our relationship in the closet for a few months more. I feared disapproval from my colleagues and possibly even repercussions from those higher up.

The friends at the reception were those who had been in on the secret—Nan, Herb and Maria McDougle, John and Joan Boyd, Bruce and Diane (or "Di, as I nicknamed her) Stewart. Joan was a faculty wife and also a story teller who had become a close friend. Diane was the faculty secretary who, with her hubby, had fabulous parties at their place in the country near Ada, the most fun and inventive being the auto treasure hunt (pre-geocaching), which Ben and I won. He drove, I navigated (pre-GPS), one of our better team efforts, and we earned a plastic trophy topped with a vintage car on top to prove it. Di also hosted quarterly poker parties. Herb and Maria were also wonderful hosts and, unlike me, lived in a great house for hosting—their beautiful, old home they'd picked up for a song, one of the perks of Beantown. I loved Herb's sense of humor, and his office being near mine, he was the neighbor I chatted with most often. I considered him a close friend. (Hoping to get a rise out of me, my other neighbor enjoyed telling me dirty jokes and staring at my breasts until I conspicuously ignored him and he finally left me alone.)

Nan sat in her wheelchair happily chatting with Bruce, another Southerner who used a wheelchair. Ready to eat her dinner, she had taken out her custom-made silverware with the extended handles, carried in a handmade leather pouch wherever she went. Herb and Maria had picked her up, not a minor chore considering the enormous van needed to transport our diminutive colleague required setting up two eight-foot long ramps for her to drive up into the vehicle. This severely hampered her social life, though a group of us were willing to help out. I was one of her primary back up peeps, which drew us closer, especially after an aid didn't show on a Saturday morning when she needed to be lifted from her bed onto the wheelchair and assisted with dress and toilet, as Percy and Eliot—her black-and-white cats named for fellow poets, Shelley and T. S. Eliot—looked on. Then she would patiently guide me as I pulled out pill after pill from her prescription bottles—the tiny green triangular one, the yellow hexagon, the orange square, etc. etc.—there must have been thirty of them. I was amazed she had memorized them all, but I suppose you can do what you need to when your life is at stake.

The reception site was low-key, owing to our modest budget and the lack of anything better. I later discovered that a much more elegant locale—an old hotel downtown—had just been renovated. I couldn't believe Joan, who was my consultant for all things Beantown, hadn't thought to mention it. But despite the low key accommodations and Herb's grumblings about the chintziness of a cash bar (he was fond of drink), almost everyone seemed to be enjoying themselves well enough.

Everyone, that is, except maybe my parents, who sat off by themselves with other members of my family. Only my outgoing brother made the effort to mingle with my in-laws, who to their credit tried to engage my parents. Ben's parents were blue collar folks. His dad, who resembled Archie Bunker in both bigotry and dress (white socks and suspenders included), not to mention crankiness, had been an auto worker at International Harvester. Marrying quite young, his mother had never finished high school. But she was a very friendly and fun-loving woman who, despite our religious differences, did her best to embrace me. I always said that, as a Christian, she walked the talk. Although my mother's own father had also been a blue collar worker, she was a snob, as my brother's wife, also from a blue collar family, knew all too well.

Ben had put some music tapes together to play during the reception. But instead of me, he picked his niece, Christy, for the first dance. I was flabberghasted. I assumed everyone knew the protocol—the bride and groom have the first dance. Right? Or sometimes perhaps a younger bride and her father, who then hands her off to her new hubby. And I was pretty sure Ben knew this, too. Was this faux pas a sign of things to come?

IN THE THREE years I'd taught at the Twig, I'd grown attached to both my colleagues and my students, some of whom I managed to inspire. There was the young man from the Brit Lit class Nathan had been in who thanked me for helping him and his friends and wanted to teach high school English after he graduated. There was the young lesbian woman who confided in me and appreciated my support. Betty from my African Am class, herself a middle-aged African American woman, was a joy to know, as was Mary Claire Stone, from both that class and women's lit. And Dana, a mentee who revised papers until she reached perfection, was an English prof's dream. These and many others made me feel part of the Twig community.

And then there were my rebels, Jack and Josh, two young Punk anarchists from the "American Rebels" class I created (Ah, what an ingenious move on my part!), who acknowledged me on the 45 their band cut, though I wasn't sure what I'd done to deserve the recognition. I had attended one of their performances at the Union Hall in Beantown, and another on campus a week before the wedding, the night Ben had his bachelor party, which somehow seemed appropriate. The front man was Jack (a.k.a., Dog Chain, as his classmates secretly called him for the choke chain he wore around his neck), also the lead singer and song writer. Josh played guitar and also wrote songs. In class, they were my rebels incarnate—the provocateurs, hell raisers, and incorrigible shit stirrers. The anarchy course I took at the Peace & Justice Center in Bloomington and the Anarchist Youth Federation convention I had attended in Yellow Springs before moving to Beantown (both on a lark) had earned me cred. That and letting them get away with far too much.

How on earth had they had managed to book the campus cafeteria, and serve beer there to boot? Jack, himself under aged, slipped me a draft behind his back. Later, they dedicated a song to me about Lucy Ricardo pleading with Ricky. *Ricky, can I go to the show? Ricky, can I go to the show?* I met Jack's mother, who I guessed was about my age. "I've heard a lot about *you,*" she said. *Really?* No mosh pit, but someone had thrown a pop can at Jack's head and he was whining it about it to his mother like a little boy wanting his mommy to kiss a boo boo. The big baby. What a difference from his badass persona. At the end, the boys opened two large garbage bags full of stuffed animals that they tore to shreds with iconoclastic glee, annihilating the innocent little critters. It hurt to watch, and I felt sorry for the maintenance guys who had to clean up the mess. But the high energy of the event—driven by the crazy fast playing of their little drummer, the Notorious S.M.A.L.L.—had me buzzing by the time I left. *How could anyone play that fast?* Maybe he guzzled high test coffee and ate fifty Snickers bars before performances like punk drummer Bill Stevenson claims he did.

I had discovered other, more conventional cultural offerings in Beantown on occasion, such as the Alvin Ailey Dance Troupe performance at the civic center or the annual Pow Wow Nan loved going to. Academic conferences took me out of town fairly often, and an old grad school friend and I made a point of meeting up at one at least once a year. Sometimes, Ben and I would venture out of town with Herb and Maria for more interesting fare than the restaurants in Beantown could offer—to Findlay for Greek food or Leipsic for authentic Mexican, craved by Maria whose dad was from Mexico. All of these memories ran through my mind as I talked with our guests and surveyed the room, grateful for all the friends I had made.

WE HONEYMOONED ON Kelleys Island on Lake Erie so Mandy could come with us. It was off season, with only one restaurant open, the weather now dreary and cold, as one would expect on the lake, the landscape gray and barren. But the small house we rented for the week was cozy and quiet, with deer munching on trees in the front yard.

We took Mandy for long walks, lounged in full-length Kaftans I'd ordered from the J. Peterman catalog, made love, rested. After the flurry of wrapping up the quarter and preparing for the wedding, I couldn't seem to get enough sleep and felt sluggish for most of the honeymoon. I noticed later in the photos we took that my face looked puffy.

"Give me a cigarette," I said to Ben one evening as we sat around talking.

"Oh no, I'm not going to be the one who starts you up again," he said. I hadn't had a cigarette in three years.

"Just one," I pleaded. "I won't start again. I promise." Who was I kidding?

"Okay."

I would stick to one a day for a while, then more, until eventually I was back to my pack-a-day habit.

On the last day, we went in search of the glacial grooves, one of the main attractions on the island. It was chilly so we bundled up. I wore the brown second-hand fedora Ray had given me, crown punched outward instead of creased. It was triple-x beaver, as Ray had pointed out, great for light drizzle and snow flurries. I would continue to wear it for decades to come. I also wore a blue wool jacket with a Southwestern design, given to me by the colleague I briefly dated my first quarter at the Twig, who had also proposed. Both remnants of relationships long past.

The grooves were long troughs etched into stone as the glacier retreated over 14,000 years ago. They were a monument to time immemorial—a sharp contrast to the short life span of all things human: a triple-x beaver hat that would last for decades but not for centuries; passion and desire (like mine for Ray); a lasting marriage—till death or divorce; the Beantown angel and the churchyard she knelt upon; a position at the Twig.

We paused to look at the enduring grooves not knowing what our own future would bring.

Subalterns

The marginalized often feel drawn to cemeteries: Outsiders, eccentrics, uneasy residents in the land of Alien Nation, those who lament the current state of affairs.

Typically, the cemetery itself sits on the outskirts of town, a place apart—a place others would rather not be reminded of.

Like draws like. We feel at home here.

Affliction

WHO WAS MARY Baker? And what happened to her?

So often during my stint as an assistant professor on the tenure track, I would find myself drawn to the back corner of the cemetery, where she is buried. It is the oldest and most remote section of the cemetery, the one most vulnerable to vandals. And until I learned its history, I thought it oddly misplaced: the dates on the stones predated Woodlawn's founding in 1873, yet they sat beyond even those most recently erected. Then I discovered it had been moved not once but twice before ending up in the back corner of Woodlawn. Or at least the markers had been relocated—most likely *without* the bodies.

Many of the stones there are that wonderful creamy white that glistens in the sun, turning a warm, rosy orange near sunset. Others, like Mary's, are sandstone, which tends to crumble and is a flat taupy brown, easy to overlook. The epitaphs in the corner are more elaborate than the others, the florid script more ornate and harder to make out. And rarely did I bother. Unlike most people who have the cemetery bug, I wasn't there for "the history." But one day, I made the effort to decipher Mary's. And I found it haunted me. *She* haunted me.

What afflicted Mary? Was she widowed at a young age, left destitute with half a dozen children to somehow provide for? No evidence of that. Perhaps she never married and ended up the penniless and much derided spinster aunt who knitted socks in exchange for her keep in her brother's home. Maybe she was sickly and fragile and suffered untold, excruciating pain. She certainly died young.

Ah, but wasn't I assuming that Mary's affliction was brought on by some external force? When I heard the word *affliction*, I couldn't help but think of Mary Rowlandson and her captivity narrative, which I taught every fall. That Mary longed for it so that, good Puritan woman that she was, she might know God loved her. And when the Indians captured her, she got the affliction she had craved and was grateful. Well, at least in hindsight. Personally, I thought she had her moments of doubt. But Mary R. was a tough, stalwart woman—a survivor—which, clearly, Mary B. was not. No, I didn't think Mary Baker's affliction was external; the inscription suggested—no, *screamed*—internal affliction, internal suffering. It was her *head*—with its "achings and thinkings"— that was "languishing." Something of a psychological nature made her breast "heave."

I pictured Mary high-strung and sensitive, hypochondriacal and melancholic, if not downright depressed. I imagined her, by turns, agitated and weeping in the flower garden and lying half-catatonic on her bed, indisposed to any who may call. Perhaps her unhappy state was triggered by the ill treatment of some uncouth suitor or rakish ne'er-do-well. Perhaps she was *seduced* and left to languish in ruin for the rest of her 29 years, 6 months and 22 days, her heart broken beyond repair. But maybe I wasn't giving Mary enough credit, taking her epitaph at face value. Perhaps on those days in the garden, sitting among the deep pink hollyhocks and the lavender irises, Mary was a "poetess" or wanted to be. Or perhaps in her most private communings with her heart, she secretly felt stymied by the Cult of True Womanhood, out of place among the submissive and pious ladies of her day, a rebel without means of expression or outlet. I liked to think of Mary as a closet rebel. Whatever her affliction, it must have distracted her from all else, left her dysfunctional, robbed her of her life.

And I wondered, *How does it feel to be remembered as a bundle of heaving affliction? How does it feel, Mary, to have others, however sympathetic and well-meaning, chalk up your life as one big mistake? to all but say, on your very tombstone, that you are better off dead?*

MARY BAKER'S HEADSTONE made me uneasy. I was well past twenty nine, and I didn't think my life as useless as Mary's, nor did I think myself nearly as neurotic nor as morbidly depressed, but I, too, had been afflicted for far too many days of my life. Too much of my time had been consumed by achings and thinkings, by neurotic anxiety and distraught languishing. Was I so different from Mary? I didn't think so. At least a part of me was like her, or the portrait I had conjured of her. No wonder she haunted me.

Did other women in academia feel the quiet desperation I felt? If so, they weren't talking about it. They weren't letting even the faintest squint of dissatisfaction cross their faces. And as I imagined Mary must have experienced, I felt isolated. Most of the women with whom I had regular contact had positions on the main campus of The Big State University over ninety miles away. From a distance, they appeared to have it all together.

I, on the other hand, had a position at the Twig, and being Twig faculty was not unlike being buried in that remote corner of Woodlawn Cemetery where poor Mary—her body and tombstone literally *un*together, most likely—lay.

> Here lies . . . *me*, stuck in a corner
> where I don't belong.
> My epitaph obscure and hard to read,
> ornate but shallow
> on crumbling sandstone.
> A flat taupy brown,
> easy to overlook.

With the hope of *not* being overlooked, I periodically made trips down to B. S. U. proper, where I felt out of place, an unhappy state triggered by ill treatment, albeit said treatment was more often than not subtle. After all, this was the enlightened and litigious nineties, when one had to be most careful not to belittle one's inferiors or women either, for that matter, in too obvious a way. Yet none of the women I encountered there seemed to experience any difficulties, much less *affliction*.

As they rattled off the latest postmodern jargon about the glories of the "destabilization of identity" and the "decentering of the unified subject" (unabridged bullshit version: *the decentering of the humanist subject consequent upon the postmodernist critique of subjectivity)*, my feminist colleagues seemed anything but destabilized or decentered themselves. They could talk about "problematizing" women (but never men, why was that?) without batting an eye or cracking the slightest smile of irony. Of course, Patricia Smiley, the one most fluent in Pomospeak, as I called it, never smiled in any case. Lydia Miserovsky's tic of adding an affected *eh?* to the end of every other sentence may have betrayed a latent smidgen of discomfort, but I doubted it. And so, too, for the half dozen or so others with whom I met to discuss feminist theory. All seemed perfectly at home in the academic milieu. In fact, they seemed perfect, period.

I, in contrast—with no small thanks to that godawful gobbledygook I was expected to parrot myself—felt thoroughly "destabilized" and "decentered," and I could have told them it didn't feel so hot. I knew it was probably wrong-headed, but I couldn't seem to shake the idea that *some* people out there *were* together and damn near perfect, which, of course, only served to make me feel even more *un*together and *not* "at one" with myself. And I knew that, if my colleagues on Main Campus could see me in my Mary Baker moments, they would think I was ridiculous. Sometimes *I* thought I was ridiculous. Just thinking about it made my breast heave.

I LED A secret life of affliction—at least I hoped it was secret. Whenever I went shopping at one of those yuppie mega-bookstores in the city, which I almost always felt an *urgent* need to do after meetings at B. S. U., I'd enter the store casting furtive glances about me to make sure none of my perfect colleagues—and especially not Patricia Smiley, heaven forbid!—were there to witness the ridiculous act I was about to commit. Once sure I was safe from detection, I'd rush over to the self help and spirituality sections to comb the shelves for titles not yet added to my collection. *I'm Dysfunctional, You're Dysfunctional?* Nope, already had that one. *High Stress Careers and the Women Who Love Them?* Neh, had that one, too. *Create Your Reality One Day at a Time?* Score! And so on and so forth, until I had found enough to fill a large shopping bag. *How to Do It ALL (And Not Go Crazy)?* Oops, there's one I missed.

Who am I? Who is that can tell me who I am?[12]

I hoarded these books like a squirrel, my shelves spilling over with them. It was as if, like an acorn in a shell, each held some kernel of wisdom and was just waiting to be cracked open and devoured. Had Mary Baker had such a plethora of acorns at her disposal, I'm sure she would have hoarded them, too, and felt every bit as squirrelly about it as I did.

Satisfied with my cache of self-help and New Age spirituality books (which, interestingly, weren't significantly different in content), I'd muster up some professional obligation and head over to the sections on literary and feminist scholarship—my penance for the previous indulgence—and fill up another shopping bag's worth. Many of these scholarly tomes (or *tombs*, as I sometimes thought of them) would never receive much more than a glimpse, but I thought they might come in handy.

At the check-out line, more furtive glances, and then I'd fight my way through the doors with my two huge shopping bags (shouldn't a bookstore have automatic doors like they have at the supermarket?) and on through the parking lot, where I struggled to balance the sheer *weight* of these two conflicting sides of myself: the scholar and the neurotic nutcase.

SETTLED INTO THE big overstuffed chair by the window next to the treetops behind the closed door of the bedroom upstairs, I'd crack open one of these acorns and gorge on its contents. There was something comforting and satisfying—subversive, even—about indulging myself in this way. It was a ritual of self-attention, this politically incorrect act, a guilty pleasure, and it allowed me to hang on to a part of myself that I couldn't acknowledge in academia. Secretly, like Mary, I felt stymied; I was a rebel without means of expression or outlet . . . a closet rebel. I may or may not have had colleagues who partook in my quiet desperation, but I knew that millions of women did. And I knew that that was significant, that there was a reason why women were obsessed with self-improvement, with remaking ourselves and creating our own reality, with healing, though we might not understand the wounds.

But alas, most of these books were simplistic and stupid, formulaic and pat, and once read, they often made me feel worse. They aggravated my affliction. They made me feel *less* competent, *less* capable of creating my own reality, *less* in control of my life. I kept thinking I should have more control. And I wasn't sure I bought the basic premise of New Age thought. Could you really create your own reality? Sure, maybe you could choose your *response* to your circumstances—and how was that for rhetorical sleight of hand?—but wasn't that almost beside the point? What about the people who were truly afflicted with abject poverty or some other nearly insurmountable circumstance? And what about *death*? "You're gonna die some day," I wanted to shout at those authors. "YOU'RE GONNA DIE! Do you think you can control *that* reality?" Several years later after moving to Columbus, I would be told that I was "underestimating" myself when I suggested this to a group of New Agers.

That there might be something wrong with *my* circumstances or that my profession didn't suit me as well as it should have were not thoughts I allowed myself to entertain. After all, compared to being poverty-stricken, wasn't it a privilege to be an academic, however tenuously? And besides, hadn't I invested an awful lot of time and money in my career? And didn't I love teaching? Yes, yes, yes. Surely there was something wrong with *me*. My *affliction* proved it, did it not? I only needed to adjust better to the demands of my career, to change. So, despite the fact that my little acorns offered little nourishment, I kept consuming them, munching on them. They were all I had. Of course, this was something like an alcoholic self-medicating with another bottle of gin.

SOMETIMES WHEN I read, I wished God would come through the window and gently shake me by the shoulder and whisper in my ear, *Kathleen, I will tell you who you are.* But even if God had drifted through my window to reveal myself to me, would it have changed my life? (Of course, this reflected "essentialist" thinking, which was frowned upon.)

I imagined Mary as wanting to write because that what was what I wanted. But my profession required me to write about what other women wrote. And as I lounged on the patio next to my own deep pink hollyhocks and lavender irises, trying to eke out chapters for my own scholarly tome/*tomb* on women's literature, doing even that was beginning to seem all but impossible. The word "women" had become *problematized* to such an extent that it is difficult to use without *scare* quotes and/or a lengthy string of qualifiers, even when writing about myself... I am a white, middle-class, predominantly heterosexual, Euro-American "woman" of leftist leanings, raised Protestant—specifically Methodist—but currently in the market for a new spiritual framework, with an apparent psychological *disability* when it comes to coping with Academia!

Who am I? Who is it that can tell me who I am?

I might not have been agitated and weeping in the flower garden, but this "woman" problem was disconcerting enough, if only because it made it hard to speak of what women might have in common. *Was* it no longer possible to delineate a tradition in women's literature, as I was trying to do, even if one took the differences among us into account? So it seemed. I searched through the scholarship I purchased at the mega-bookstore for theories that would lift me out of the postmodern abyss, but without success.

I had a pernicious case of the anxiety of authorship. The idea was now considered passé, yet there I was, proof that "women's" anxiety of authorship was still alive, thank you very much, in the late twentieth century.

And speaking of *The Madwoman in the Attic*, so named for Bertha Rochester in *Jane Eyre*, the madwoman in my own attic would occasionally erupt with a vengeance. This usually happened in the mornings of yet another frantic work day, when my Inner Bertha had had enough. I HATE MY LIFE! I HATE MY LIFE! I HATE MY F*%?ING LIFE! she'd scream through the house. But then my Inner Jane would calmly say that I needed to create my own reality with an attitude adjustment. *Just SUBMIT*, she'd say. *SUBMIT* to all you have to do. *It'll be easier* *that way.* And wasn't Jane right? Wasn't it always best to cope with *trying circumstances* in a sane and measured way?

I filled dozens of journals with resolutions. Lists and lists of goals and how I was going to better discipline myself to accomplish them. Prescriptions galore, gleaned from my reading, to cure what ailed me, to "fix" myself, to better fit into the not-so-Sacred Groves of Academe. The verbal equivalent of agitation and weeping. Anguish about not being good enough. Anxious scribblings hidden between the covers of pretty flowers and lovely nineteenth-century paintings of ladies sitting in gardens. Ladies, perhaps, like Mary. *(How does it feel to be a bundle of heaving affliction? How does it feel to chalk up your life as one big mistake?)* And lurking beneath my anguish? A subtext of dark *foreboding* that, no matter what I did, I wouldn't make tenure anyway.

THIS FOREBODING BEGAN my second year when Nan and I visited Main Campus for a workshop on Jim Reaper's unintentionally disturbing paper on *Beloved,* where we hoped to wow them with our astute observations. On the trip down in her van, we had a high old time critiquing the hell out of Reaper's paper. Academic discourse aside, it read like a Harlequin bodice-ripper, with "the text" as prospective rape victim—and a black one at that—a dreadful implication to which Reaper, in all his white manliness, was deplorably oblivious.

"He makes his desire to 'enter' and 'penetrate' the 'resistant' novel sound like a rape fantasy," I'd scoffed.

To which Nan had tittered with glee. She despised Reaper's smugness, along with that of most of our colleagues on Main Campus, almost as much as I did. Because we were regional faculty, they assumed themselves to be superior to us.

"And there's something not quite right about the way he shifts gears," I added, groping my way toward understanding, as I do. "He's stuck in a subject-object dichotomy, then seems to want to shift toward a paradigm of multiplicity but without quite recognizing what he's doing, which seems pretty lame for a theorist."

"Oh, that's *good,*" Nan gloated. "We're going to impress the hell out of them."

"Well, I don't think we should mention the rape part," I replied.

And of course we didn't. But silly us for thinking they wanted to be impressed by our keen intellect.

During the workshop, I watched aghast as one feminist after another kowtowed to Reaper, almost fawningly. Not one alluded to his rapist mentality, not even in subtle, face-saving terms. Playing the grande dame, Marcy Longaberger had even patted Reaper on the back, saying perhaps Annie, his wife, had been a positive influence on his awareness of being a male reader. *Seriously?* Nan and I exchanged surreptitious glances. *Why were they were handling him with kid gloves?* What did they know that we didn't?

Afterward, the sole black woman in the department—only recently recruited from a nearby college and no doubt very astute about workplace politics—walked up to us and said, in the most congenial way, "My, you two sure have a lot to say! I'll have to get you to read my work sometime." But her eyes relayed the deeper message: *This is a game you need to learn how to play if you're going to survive.* It was then I realized my faux pas: What was expected was not my participation—astute or otherwise—but my silence.

A year later, Reaper became departmental chair. When word reached the Twig, I could almost hear the Fates snickering at my rotten luck. After that, this morose, bony man treated me with chilly disregard. He conveniently overlooked several sets of my most positive student evaluations without apology. For the annual reviews of my work, he deliberately picked the most obnoxious people he could find to assist— such as the deceptively cute Lil Appledumpling, who assumed the role of departmental pit bull (bet they rue the day they recruited her!)— and then they bombarded me with questions as if I were a graduate student in an oral exam, to which I clumsily responded with stuttering *ineptitude*.

And so, there were reasons—compelling ones—for my forebodings. But what else could I do but carry on? Maybe *affliction* was just another word for a premonition you didn't know what to do with.

Someday, when this ordeal was over, I resolved to box up those stupid little books I read—lay them to rest in cardboard caskets!—and banish them from my life. And I would shed nary a tear for their passing! In the meantime, however, I dared not stop trying to *pull myself together*, though frankly, I was beginning to think it was a lost cause.

Had Monsieur Academe seduced me like some uncouth suitor or rakish ne'er-do-well, leaving me half-catatonic . . . left to languish in ruin, broken beyond repair?

THE LEAVES OF the maple tree overhead, a blazing vermilion mere weeks before, had since faded to a dusty mauve. Had Mary walked in the cemetery, too? I imagined her walking in late autumn, kicking the dry, dying leaves with her boot, her voluminous skirt rustling, as she inhaled their sharp, spicy scent to calm her frazzled nerves. How ironic that decay smelled so sweet.

A row back and several markers over from Mary's was a white marble stone, featuring a bas-relief of a woman's bust. I walked over for a closer look. Etched into the stone in large block letters beneath her image was her name: LAMENTA. *Lamenta!* Who on earth would give their child such a dreary name, all but condemning her to a life of sorrow and regret? For this staid woman had once been a child, though it was hard to imagine when looking at the carved rendition of her face. The face was placid yet stern. Her hair was pulled back tight from her face in a bun, her dress buttoned all the way up to her neck. She had been pious, no doubt, a True Woman. There was a severity about her, reminiscent of Patricia Smiley, and strength, too, which was admirable, though it was the strength of endurance rather than defiance. And there was a coldness about her as well. Even when alive, you could be fairly certain, she had had a persona carved in stone. What *laments* had Lamenta lamented? Had she taken them with her to her grave? Whatever Lamenta's story, her monument didn't tug at my heart the way Mary's faceless stone did.

How does it feel to be remembered as a bundle of heaving affliction? How does it feel to have others chalk up your life as one big mistake?

My thoughts turned away from the lives of Lamenta and Mary, back to my own and the day we women at the Twig had discussed *Women Who Run with the Wolves* together. I had ended up lying down on the couch in the faculty lounge—hand on languishing forehead—complaining about my life, wanting a therapy session . . . *I don't run with the wolves,* I thought, *I lie with them. I don't howl with the wolves, I whimper and whine.* Yet I hadn't always been this way. I used to have that strength of defiance. I used to have a burning flame inside. But somewhere along the way, the flame just sort of sputtered and died . . .

I am 40 years, 6 mo.

& 10 days old,

and I am *tired.*

Something must be wrong.

Broken Vessel

I am forgotten as a dead man out of mind:
I am like a broken vessel.
For I have heard the slander of many:
*   fear was on every side:*
*   while they took counsel together against me,*
*   they devised to take away my life.*
*   Psalms 31:9*

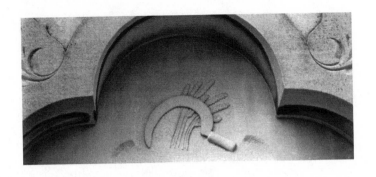

Reaper's Hook

Because I could not stop for Death,
He kindly stopped for me;
The carriage held but just ourselves
And Immortality.

~ Emily Dickinson

THE REAPER ISN'T always cloaked in a long black robe and cowl. His hook isn't always a scythe. Him-with-the-Square-Toes may wear a tweed jacket with suede patches at the elbows, or blue jeans and a striped Oxford shirt. He may sport longish hair and a beard, have a host of young acolytes trotting after him, hoping to hear him play a few strains on his guitar—some Dylan perhaps—at the departmental picnic. (You will watch and wonder at his appeal.) Very likely, he will be tall and gaunt, morose and self-assured. The sort of man who ambles. You will notice that his peers are careful in how they speak to or about him. That dogs run from him, though cats may rub up against his leg. That he is never careless or messy, except when it suits his purpose.

No, he may not always be what you expect. But always, always he dirties his hands in destiny, executing his will both near and far, secretly rubbing his hands in glee. For your livelihood is his harvest, your bloody disappointment the nightcap he sips before going to bed.

ON AN AFTERNOON in the October following my Ralph Edwards Moment in Woodlawn (*I'm going to write about this!*), I awaited my call from destiny in the form of Professor Jim Reaper, who would inform me whether the senior professoriate had decided to grant me tenure. My future hinged on the outcome: It would be up or out for me.

I had been waiting all afternoon, staring out the living room window at autumn's changing leaves, filled with apprehension. I had made it over the hurdle at my own campus in Beantown. Impressed with my teaching and satisfied with my service record, the Twig had approved my being tenured. Now it was up to the senior English Department faculty on the main campus and tenured profs from the regionals—which included only O'Malley and Schmidt from the Twig to represent me—to approve on the basis of my research, before my case moved up the administrative chain of command.

Albeit unfinished, the three-hundred-page manuscript of *The Green Letter* I'd submitted might not have been cutting edge, but it was solid and important. Reviews from scholars outside of B.S.U. were positive overall, and several publishers had expressed interest in publishing it. In addition, I had presented numerous conference papers and published a few articles. And a year and a half earlier, I had made it through the fourth-year review with a nearly unanimous vote of confidence from my colleagues on Main Campus. However, due to complications here and there and running out of time for an overly ambitious project (but shouldn't breadth and ambition count for something?), not to mention putting way too much time into teaching, I hadn't been able to finish by the deadline. And it didn't help that the requirements had changed a few years after I was hired from having a publishable manuscript to a completed one with a contract lined up.

What troubled me most, however, was my arch nemesis, Reaper himself. As department chair, he had the power to steer the course of my fate, and of course, we had had a number of grim encounters. I thought back to my second year and the infamous *Beloved* incident, the workshop I'd attended featuring Reaper's unintentionally disturbing paper on the novel, my unsavvy handling of the situation, and the fact that Reaper became department chair the next year.

And then, the following year, there was that annual review with Reaper and departmental pit bull, Lil Appledumpling. *Grim, grim, grim.* And maybe it wouldn't have been, if only I had been more strategic and given them the published article on Hurston that everyone seemed to like, or the book's chapter based on it as a sample to discuss. Something polished. But *noooo*, I had to give the latest chapter I'd been working on and felt excited about, the one explaining the green letter, hoping not only that it would impress them but also that I might actually get some useful feedback. So like me. So *not* shrewd. *So utterly clueless.* Not just green but *chartreuse!*

Lew Brooks, chair of the promotion and tenure committee and a noted creative writer, had been impressed with it, actually. When we chatted outside of Reaper's office, he was friendly and encouraging.

"I'm a little nervous," I confided. *Never let 'em see me sweat, Stupid!*

"Oh, I'm sure it will go well, Kathy," he'd said as he ushered me into Reaper's office.

But having seen which way the wind blew during the meeting, Lew turned cool toward me forever after. The lack of loyalty and backbone among colleagues is appalling but predictable.

"Well, I want to know what you mean by 'women,'" Lil taunted. "Surely there were women of color writing about nature during the early nineteenth century." But for the most part, there weren't. Phillis Wheatley aside, very few women of color had either the literacy or the leisure to write, much less the privilege to publish, in the pre-Civil War period.

"How do you define 'pastoral'?" Reaper interrogated next. A legitimate enough question, of course, but asked in such a belligerent manner, it made me feel like I was defending my dissertation all over again—though my profs had been a lot more respectful. Instead, he could have treated me like a colleague and used my explanation in the chapter as a springboard for discussing it. (I had ended up reworking Leo Marx's classic paradigm of the Machine in the Garden into the Phallus in the Garden, which was used to subversively critique and exclude male characters who exhibited dominance or aggression.) In his official write up of the review, Reaper managed to make it sound as if I were an imbecile who didn't understand her own topic.

If only I were better on my feet. If only. If only. If only . . .

If only I didn't suck at promoting myself and my work.

And how had he managed to exclude nearly *half* of my highest scoring student evaluations? And more importantly, *why* had he done it? He who was not known to be careless or disorganized or even unfair. Sure seemed suspicious.

And then, I'd made the mistake of offering a compliment that he'd ended up using against me. It came before the debriefing of my fourth-year review, when Reaper said he needed to finish putting away some files before we began. "That's impressive," I'd said in an effort to be friendly. "I should be as organized as you are!" Next thing I knew, in his summary letter for my file, he noted that I was "disorganized."

Reaper was retaliating. I was sure of it.

And *then* (ah, so many *and then*'s in this melodrama!), there was the strange incident that had happened in the special topics course I had created and taught on Main Campus all because none of them had been willing to drive the ninety miles up to Beantown to observe my teaching for the fourth-year review (my Beantown colleagues deemed insufficient). "Cultural Intersections," the special topics course, had been described in Longaberger's evaluation as one of the best classes she'd ever seen anywhere, noting that my way of handling discussion was magical. But somewhere along the way, a small group of serious students, led by an overzealous ringleader with a self-righteous, bad-ass complex, decided to be angry at me for not being able to force a recalcitrant student to do the reading. They described themselves as sitting in the corner in protest. What was I supposed to do, visit the girl's dorm room and stand over her like a fascist nun with a ruler poised to thwamp her knuckles every time she looked up from the page? Inviting her to drop the course would have been frowned upon by the university. At any rate, this situation resulted in the lowest student evaluation score I'd ever received. I doubted those voting on my case cared all that much about the quality of my teaching anyway, but I suspected that, if they didn't want me, they'd use anything they could against me. The whole mess was exasperating.

And how ridiculous that I had to teach three courses down there for an entire quarter, driving 180 miles' round trip twice a week for ten weeks (3,600 miles total)—time and energy surely better spent doing research—so they could evaluate my teaching of *their* students on *their* campus. Never mind that my students were different from theirs, with different needs; that many were older, had children and jobs; had special challenges, including poverty, to deal with; that many were the first in their families or among their friends to attend college. Because of the fast-approaching deadline for the fourth-year review (the first up-or-outer), I had to have them observe me within the first two weeks of classes, just I was getting acquainted with the students. Ironically, Lew harassed me about getting these in earlier until I reminded him of the circumstances.

I WAS GETTING antsy. It was getting late and still no call from Reaper. Probably not a good sign.

Just as the sun bent down to kiss the horizon good evening, the phone finally rang.

"Hi, Kathy. This is Jim Reaper." His voice sounded somber, but then it always did.

"Yes?"

"I'm sorry. The senior faculty voted not to grant you tenure."

"Oh. What was the breakdown?" I tried to hide my reaction even though I felt like my guts had just been ripped out.

"Nearly unanimous. One voted for you, five abstained, the rest against. Please call Susan to schedule a follow-up meeting so we can discuss it in detail." *Bang, bang, you're dead. Please schedule your own autopsy.*

"Yes. Okay. Thank you."

The rejection hurt. But I did not cry, at least not yet. Instead, a little voice inside me cheered, *I'm free! I'm free!*

BUT I DID cry the next morning.

The breakdown of the vote meant that at least one of my own—O'Malley or Schmidt, the only two profs from Beantown—had not voted on my behalf. I suspected Schmidt, who had little sense of loyalty and probably little courage to go against the colleagues on Main Campus whose approval he so desperately craved. I could imagine him, sheeplike, baaing a "Nay" along with the majority at my review to show he was one of them. That left O'Malley, who I believed was capable of standing alone as the sole supporter. I dismissed the possibility that either bore a grudge over the Nathan incident; both had simply been too supportive of my work in the years since.

The breakdown also revealed that the department's feminists had not come to my defense either; somehow this hurt me most of all. But how to explain the complete reversal of nearly unanimous approval at the fourth-year review to near unanimous *dis*approval a mere year and a half later? It was a case of group think, obviously. But how does that *happen*?

I imagined surreptitious whispering in hallways in the weeks before they met officially behind closed doors to discuss my case. But that seemed unlikely if only because it was doubtful they cared enough about Twig faculty to bother. I thought it also unlikely that most would have bothered to read the book manuscript or even the articles I'd submitted. No, they'd have been more inclined to have listened to the two who had read at least part of it—initially at my request, as urged by Schmidt, to get feedback and to make a connection: Sarah Bighead, the current golden girl of the department, who questioned my acceptance of Gilbert and Gubar's thesis, which she felt had been "disproven," as if literary theories have criteria equal to scientific ones; and Beatrice Flowers, a senior colleague from another regional campus, who had asked me to provide her with a reading list of feminist criticism so she could *begin* to understand the chapter I'd given her to read and whose own book was so completely lacking in substance or originality I found it hard to have much respect for her opinion of mine. Which had not been shared with me privately, by the way. *Geez!* Comments relayed during the autopsy with Reaper confirmed the group's blind reliance on these two figures.

Why hadn't I realized this might happen? That the two people I'd asked to read a sampling of my work would not only be called upon to testify for or against me but also serve as the sole "witnesses"? Stupid, stupid, stupid.

And again, how stupid that I'd given these witnesses the least seasoned chapters to read!

The glowing reviews from peers outside of B.S.U. were written off completely with flimsy excuses and half-assed assumptions. *The most famous one probably hadn't read it; that one used to teach on the Beantown campus and was therefore biased,* etc. The negative one was latched onto, its political agenda completely overlooked. Fearing that it would offend men, my critic clearly wanted to distance herself from the subversive ways in which my authors used the pastoral to punish or exclude aggressive male characters. My English colleagues on Main Campus dismissed nearly all of my scholarship. That my chapter on Margaret Fuller was selected to be presented at the Modern Language Association Convention—normally a coup, especially for junior faculty—hadn't meant much to them. Nor had the other fifteen presentations I'd given in five years. Or the talks to the community. Or the articles I'd published.

Regarding the weird incident in the Cultural Intersections class, I was charged with "blaming the students" for my low score. Would blaming myself have worked any better to my advantage? *Don't think so.*

Most of the university presses that had expressed interest in publishing the book were dismissed as second tier because they were Southern, though only a year or two before, this had been adequate for another regional campus colleague to get tenure. The more prestigious University of Illinois Press was blown off as well.

I later heard that John Owens, one of the junior English faculty on Main Campus, had been granted tenure for far fewer accomplishments than mine.

"Why?" I asked my informant.

"He was calling in his markers."

"What does that mean?"

"Because he was from Yale, he knows important people. He made connections with them for the folks on Main Campus."

"Oh."

It took me a minute to pick my jaw up off the floor. John *was* affable and even admitted to being slow, but the favoritism on his behalf was so blatant it was shocking. So agreed the Dean of Arts & Science who, in a very rare move, reversed the department's pass.

I didn't have anything like John had to bring to the table. And I just wasn't very skilled at playing politics anyway. I had tried to make connections on Main Campus, had tried to socialize, though inadequately with the limited energy I had to put into it. None of it had been enough to help me over the edge of acceptance.

"FUCK 'EM," BEN said later on the day that Reaper called. "You did the best you could, and your best should've been good enough. For what it's worth, *I* believe in you."

"Thanks, Ben." His support would mean a lot in the months to come.

"Well, it's their loss. You are the best professor I ever had."

That weekend, we went home to Gallipolis to visit my parents and brother.

I half expected Dad to say, "You don't know how to play the game," to blame me as he had for the fiasco of my year in hell where the discrimination couldn't have been more blatant. Or my brother to say, "You don't know how to kiss up," which amounted to the same thing as not playing the game, as far as I could tell. But both had the good sense not to say either that weekend. Everyone was sympathetic, though not profusely so.

Dan wondered if marrying a student had worked against me.

"I really don't think so," I said. "I passed on the Beantown campus, and I doubt the folks on Main Campus even knew about it. Besides, it's not uncommon for male profs to marry their students."

It would have been nice to have heard something like, "We still love you anyway." But sometimes you just have to just latch on to what you're given.

SHOULD I APPEAL the decision? I briefly considered the option but was so exhausted from the process and my demise, I didn't have it in me. Besides, I didn't feel confident in a favorable outcome. After all, I hadn't finished the book manuscript, as was required. However, sometime later, a friend of mine said they could have given me an extension if they'd really wanted to.

And so, my tenure track had come to a dead end. In the Graveyard of Academe, I had come to the sign that said NO THRU TRAFFIC. I could turn around and start all over again at a different institution or even leave the graveyard and look for a different path altogether. But in the meantime, all I could manage was to sit there before deciding what to do and where to go next. Having been reaped, I now had to glean what I could from the last five years.

Sleep of the Dead

AS WITH SLEEP, the deceased go heavy. Dead weight. The spirit is gone; the light, extinguished. There is no energy to animate. The spirit has separated from its house of flesh and fluid, bone and blood. It has risen, moved on to other worlds, or sunk into the earth to feed a crocus in springtime. The earth grounds the spirit of the living like a magnet holding it in place; the stars welcome it home. But the spirit of the living dead is confused, weary with struggle.

"Kathy, you're so listless." That's what Ivo said to me, almost shocked, when he stuck his head in my office door. I didn't think it showed. But he was right: I was so very tired, so overwhelmed with fatigue that it was all I could do to prep my classes and tend to the bare minimum of duties. I gulped down vitamins and herbs as if they were an elixir. I slept. I took Mandy for walks. I tried to eat well. But nothing seemed to help. My body was so heavy, you would have thought weights were tied to my limbs. I was utterly and profoundly exhausted. Mentally, physically, emotionally. Through and through, to the very marrow of my bones. I was listless, lifeless.

After years of living on adrenaline, I suppose this makes sense. But I'd never experienced anything like it. Was I depressed? Or simply drained? I wanted to know. But the only answer I had was that heaviness, that weariness. Go down, my body said. Lie down, succumb to it. Rest in peace. And I had no choice but to obey.

Stop Clock, Cover Mirror

Curtains would be drawn and clocks would be stopped at the time of death. Mirrors were covered with crape or veiling to prevent the deceased's spirit from getting trapped in the looking glass.

~ "Victorian Funeral Customs,"
Friends of Oak Grove Cemetery

NEAR HALLOWEEN, AS Mandy and I were strolling in Woodlawn, I stopped to admire a large Catalpa in a section not far from the gate. Its leaves had turned a soft golden yellow, and enough of them had fallen to expose the tree's gnarly branches, its crooked bones. In autumn, it was the spookiest tree in the cemetery. The kind you half expected to snarl at you like the disgruntled apple trees in *The Wizard of Oz*. Or at least that's what you might half expect in October, the gothiest month of the year. In the fall, I had always loved walking in Woodlawn as a backdrop to teaching "The Legend of Sleepy Hollow," "Young Goodman Brown," Poe's "Raven." But now, it brought me little pleasure, and striking a little too close to home, the wisecracking raven's mantra of *Nevermore!* no longer amused me. These days, nothing much did.

Who was I now? With no reflection from others besides pity or survivor's guilt, I was no longer sure. The tenure clock had stopped, and while I went on teaching and tending to daily business in some minimal fashion, there was no more ticking to drive me through the days with such breathless urgency as before. Though I had never felt like a professor as most people think of it, I guess it was a larger part of my identity than I had realized. Certainly, it was part of my pride.

Metaphorically, my situation was not unlike the old folk custom of stopping the clocks and covering the mirrors when someone dies. For the dead, time has stopped. No reflection looks back from the silver and glass to tell them who they are. In my case, the image of "Professor Davies" was now veiled.

The difference between the folk practice and the version of it in academia, however, is respect. This is seen in the classic film *Fried Green Tomatoes,* which was based on the novel I taught while on the track. When Sipsey stops the clock and covers the mirrors after Ruth's death, you can feel the respect she has for Ruth in the act. Not so in Academe, no siree. No apparent sadness for your passing even, at least not by higher-ups. The clock stops by default (do not pass go, do not collect $200), and the mirror is covered by you own abject confusion.

To comfort the grieving Idgy, Sipsey says, "Miss Ruth was a lady, and a lady always knows when to leave." This was something I had never been especially good at. At parties, Ben and I were usually among the last to leave. While he talked endlessly, I would get all settled in and comfy until inertia and complacency set in, leaving me careless about manners. I guess I am no lady. But this had been no party, and livelihood was still at stake. Having nowhere to go, I was in no hurry to leave.

Which was a good thing, since I could barely walk. Within days after Reaper's call, my back had gone out. I was in the women's room (shades of Marilyn French) when I bent down to pick up my briefcase, heavy with the three-inch, pre-Civil War volume of the *Heath Anthology of American Literature*—damn thing must've weighed ten pounds—and found I could not straighten my back. Fitting that my body should choose to mirror my life circumstances by withdrawing support and turning my pain inside out. Not knowing where to go for help, I had done nothing. Although my back had recovered to some extent, I was still creeping around a bit.

Fortunately, I didn't need to hurry very much. One of the few perks of the tenure system is that, once you're denied, you can still have the rest of that school year and the next to regroup and hopefully find another position, which of course gives your employer plenty of time to find your replacement. And while this liminal state is akin to purgatory, I was grateful to have time to reflect and reassess. Not to mention, rest.

As I stood there looking at the gnarly Catalpa, I thought of Ted Nelson, who considered suicide after being denied tenure two years before I was. The dream of being a professor was so strong in him, was such a consuming part of his identity and self-worth, that losing the prospect of it was almost more than he could bear. Thank God I hadn't invested my own identity or self-worth exclusively in being a professor. In fact, possibly influenced by what I'd seen poor Ted go through (*Alas, Poor Yorick!*), the very next day after being "reaped," I resolved not to let it destroy me. "There is much more to life than all of that," I wrote in my journal. "There is a deeper sense of life and of me. I feel that most when I can see myself as 'just a regular person.'"

But that didn't mean the tenure denial didn't affect my self-esteem, at least temporarily. If life's tragedies strengthen us, that doesn't happen overnight. A realignment is necessary, some chiropractic of the self or soul.

WE CAME TO the headstone marked DAVIES. The one that years before made me laugh, nervously, wondering what the fate of my career in Beantown would be. I shook my head and went on up the hill to the grief-stricken little lady holding a wreath, tears on the verge of falling, or so I imagined. I had only once actually shed tears, but my body seemed to be expressing my sadness through overwhelming fatigue. Or maybe it was simply exhaustion from all the effort I had expended, capped with the letdown of the outcome. Whatever the cause, it was all I could do to drag myself through the days, a condition that would only worsen in the coming months. I plied myself with vitamins and supplements but to little end. I felt like a phantom.

Some colleagues, like Ivo, my friend in the math department, commented directly on how listless I'd become. Most, of course, expressed sympathy without remarking on my state.

Nan rolled her wheel chair up to my office door and, with a pout, sat there in funereal silence. No gossip, no plot summaries, no references to past loves; just a shake of the head.

"Well, the good news is, I got my Get Out of Jail Free card," I said.

"It's not fair," she whispered.

Schmidt tried to sound upbeat.

"Well it's too bad you didn't make it. But now you need to gear up for finding a new position."

"Yeah, sure," I replied, trying not to cry. I no longer embraced his coaching. I was pretty sure he—the one who had mentored me more than anyone else—was the one hadn't voted for me. Traitor.

"Have you seen the MLA job list yet?" he asked.

Oh, please.

I had gone to O'Malley's door myself. All I had to do was stand there, eyebrows raised, grimacing before he responded.

"I'm so sorry," he said, his expression genuinely sad. "I really thought we had them. The external reviews were so good." I recalled his excitement when I had shown him the letters a few months before.

"Can you tell me what happened at the meeting?"

"No, we aren't allowed to discuss that," he said. *Did he look sheepish? Guilty?*

I knew that some senior profs did, in fact, confide what had happened behind closed doors, at least if they felt close to their protégés, but I guessed Tim wasn't going to be one of them.

Had he been the one who stood by me, or not?

The answer would come clearer a few months later when Ben ran into Tim's wife, Marian.

"She said Tim was very upset about your not getting tenure," Ben said. "I don't think he was the one who betrayed you." He looked at me pointedly. No fan of Schmidt, whom he'd had in class, he shared my suspicions that he, not O'Malley, had been the turncoat. After that, I felt more comfortable around Tim, but until then, it was awkward.

Fortunately, I could be myself in all my misery. Unlike my friend who had to face her betrayers every day on Main Campus, I had only one or two people to worry about.

I HAD TO put up some pretense for the Midwest MLA Conference only two weeks away and the MLA Convention at the end of December. I had organized a panel for the former and was to present papers at both.

Normally, presenting at MLA is a coup, especially for junior faculty, and it would shine brightly on my CV, which might still get me a decent job, even it hadn't counted for much with my colleagues at B.S.U. At MMLA, I would also be debriefed about the tenure denial by belated mentors, who had also served as external reviewers of my manuscript. At MLA, I would be meeting with an editor from Illinois University Press to discuss the advance contract for publishing my book.

Chris Evans, Schmidt's friend, had had my position at Beantown before me. Having heard so much about him, I found him easy to relate to. Our rapport was so comfortable, people thought we were old friends.

"I really think if you could get Illinois to publish your book and you could get B.S.U. to grant you a seventh-year extension, you'd have a good crack at tenure. That would put you in a stronger position to find a job elsewhere."

"Gosh, Chris, I don't know . . ." I doubted they'd give me an extension or even care if I published the book. I felt they were done with me.

"Illinois contacted me, you know."

He seemed unfazed by my shortcomings. I was touched by his willingness to suspend judgment and encouraged by his support.

I had arranged to meet Mary Barnstone Black by inviting her to be on a panel I had organized months before for the MMLA. About twenty years my senior, she was able to give me a seasoned feminist's perspective, along with some special insights into the emerging field of ecocriticism (ecological literary scholarship), which my work was a part of.

"I just don't believe it is possible for anyone doing work in that area to be accepted for tenure at this time. It's too new," she said.

Naïve little me, once again, thinking that had been a point in my favor.

"I suggest that, until you get tenure, you avoid that affiliation."

"Do you really think so?" How disheartening.

"Things are bad out there. Have you ever considered going into administration?"

"Oh God no," I replied. That would've been the last thing I would've wanted to do. I doubted I was cut out for it anyway.

Mary then told me how she had gone back to grad school late in life, after her kids were grown, and having the enthusiasm of a late bloomer who was at last following her passion, her work provided her immeasurable joy. As a feminist scholar, she had been successful, but like mine, her work spoke of women's literary traditions, which in light of the dominance of postmodern theory, was seen to be problematic. In fact, she had applied for a senior position at the B.S.U. English Department on Main Campus, but I knew she'd never get it.

"You don't seem to have had proper mentoring," she said, looking both concerned and appalled. "At least not in our field."

"No, I really haven't." Even in grad school, I'd never had a true mentor. Along with some bad luck, such as my dissertation director moving to Germany, I seemed to have neither the skills nor the magnetism needed for making connections, a situation not uncommon for women.

"That's a shame. Would you like to be one of my little kittens?"

Ugh. I nodded, but I was secretly put off. I wasn't sure I wanted to be anyone's "little kitten."

Still, it was nice to have feminist support. All those years I had dutifully attended the quarterly discussion group meetings of the English Department feminists in Columbus, hoping to establish myself in their community. Of the bunch, Lydia extended herself to me the most, occasionally asking how things were going, but my connections to the department feminists had been flimsy at best. None seemed especially interested in my work or very invested in me or my future at B.S.U.

Had a single one voted on my behalf? I doubted it, and it hurt that, ultimately, I got so little support from them. Was I wrong to have expected it?

Had any of them felt the slightest twinge of guilt?

The answer would come nearly a decade later in Bloomington at a tribute for Susan Gubar given by her former students, from a woman who started teaching at the Twig my last year there. When I was there, she had kept her distance, but now, at I.U., our alma mater, she was more open.

"I think you got the shaft," she said bluntly.

"Really?" I was surprised at her candor. "I felt let down by the feminists on Main Campus," I confided.

"I think they felt bad about what happened to you, Kathy," she said. "So they made more of an effort with me and some other women." At least my demise ended up helping others.

"Thank you for telling me that, Liz." Even though the revelation came ten years after the fact, hearing it was validating.

IN THE MEANTIME, support came from unexpected sources. Just before the denial, my former student Jack appeared at my office door, dressed in uncharacteristic conservative garb, ready to return to school. He'd been such a goof-off when younger, I had told him he was wasting his time. Now, with aspirations to go to law school, he was ready to dig in. He was still the punk anarchist I'd known before (he wore the conservative get up to impress those who would reinstate his enrollment status), and in no time, he was back in black and sporting a raging mohawk. Jack had a tough, sometimes snarling exterior and an ego the size of Texas, but he was one of the few people to actively encourage me. He took as many classes with me as he could and hung out in my office almost daily. He was also a notorious womanizer who liked to tease me on occasion, so I had to keep him in check.

For spiritual sustenance, I attended a reading group at the Unity church in Beantown for a few months, until I once again grew weary of New Age dogma. It was there I befriended Carolyn, a woman my age who would later take my women's lit class. She was the only friend I made in Beantown not affiliated with the Twig. She, too, was very supportive and kind to me.

Mandy and I walked past the monument of John C. Calvin, namesake of the building that housed the English Department at the Twig. Thinking of Jack reminded me of all the students who had appreciated me over the years. Reaper had rated my teaching as merely "good." My students and colleagues at the Twig saw my teaching differently. On our campus, I had earned a reputation for being an excellent teacher, and students were excited about taking my classes. Hyacinth had even asked me to coach a colleague in sociology who had wretched student evaluations. Twice I had been nominated for the Twig's Outstanding Teacher Award. Twice also (and a third time, later) I had been invited to the University-Wide Salute to Undergraduate Achievement Banquet. Hadn't I proven that my teaching was better than "good"?

I wondered if they cared much about teaching anyway. They seemed to use whatever they could—even downplaying your successes—to justify denying you tenure if that was what they'd decided they wanted to do.

I loved teaching, and I loved my students. I loved inspiring and encouraging them. I'd been doing it for almost twenty years. It was my calling. I didn't see myself embarking on a new career. But how hard would it be to find another position? Would I end up like Ted—teaching a gazillion courses as an adjunct for poverty wages the rest of my life?

MANDY AND I headed to the back corner to visit our old friends, Lamenta and Mary Baker. Lamenta looked on disapprovingly as I read Mary's epitaph once again.

> Her languishing head is at rest,
> Its achings and thinkings are o'er,
> This quiet immoveable breast
> Is heaved by affliction no more.

Now that I was all but dead in the eyes of the university, I wanted to believe that my own breast was heaved by affliction no more, and that, like Mary, I was better off. But I knew that wasn't the case. Not only would I still have to face finishing my book and finding a job, I would also need to recover myself. Revive the ghost I had become.

Soon, I would begin prepping a special topics course for winter quarter—"The Quest"—designed as much for me and my ghostly self as for students who might also wish to explore identity issues for themselves. I was hoping with this I might rent the veil, uncover the mirror and possibly with an *Abracadabra!* meet my new self, or rather my old truer self, and get back on a more authentic path.

We said our goodbyes to Mary B. and walked on. When we passed the sphinxes, I could swear they smirked.

In less than a week, it would be All Soul's Day, when Catholics would pray for the dead, especially those who (like me) languished in Purgatory. I would have to remember to pray for myself.

And then I looked up to see the Black monument, the light pink ribbon tied as a remembrance to one of its pillars, a careless leftover from summer. The distinguished woman on top of the pedestal gripped the anchor of hope with a dignity I found inspiring.

Madonna Dolorosa

IT WAS THE day before Easter, and as I walked in Woodlawn down the Avenue of Trees, I found myself in tears. Watching me with doggy concern, Mandy stayed close, offering protection.

It hurts. It hurts. It hurts. The phrase ran through my mind like a mantra, just as it does when you suffer a physical injury. In that case, full acknowledgement and concentration on the pain seem to help in recovery. But when the pain is psychological, the mantra can only hinder healing, keeping us stuck. I was tired of being stuck. And at that moment, I felt the full weight of my stuckness. What I carried was the burden of feeling inadequate. It seemed I had lugged it around with me my whole life. It had not served me. The awful weight of it was unbearable.

I imagined my own private Easter, as I often did in difficult times, envisioning a miraculous renewal of my spirit. A *resurrection*. Because I was born in April, springtime and especially Easter had always held personal symbolism for me. This had never been truer than it was that year. I yearned for transformation. I prayed for divine intervention to revive me.

The path I called the Avenue of Trees marked the boundary between Woodlawn and Gethsemane, the Catholic cemetery. Through the budding trees with their chartreusey promise, I saw a life-sized Pietà, with Mary holding her crucified son on her lap. But the statue was crudely wrought and ugly. In it, I found no encouragement or comfort.

That could be found beyond where I could see, in the colossal angel standing before a giant cross and the statue of Mary with her Sacred Heart, arms extended to embrace.

Ladies in Mourning,
Women with Wings

Outside the doors of study . . . an angel waits.
~ Hannah Green, 19th-C. American Writer

IT WAS JOB application time once again and only a year left on my contract, yet I wasn't at all motivated. And I couldn't have cared less if I ever wrote another word of literary scholarship, much less finished the book I'd been working on for tenure, even if the University of Illinois was waiting on the manuscript. In fact, I carried the advance contract around my neck like a stinky dead thing. Instead, I was stuck in the purgatory of post-denial and its accompanying grief over the loss. And then one morning, the Angel of Synchronicity came knocking at my door to lift me out of the doldrums.

Said angel wore the guise of Macky, a word-weary English major, almost exactly my age, who hovered on the threshold of my office wanting to do an independent study.

"I need a break from literature," she announced. "I need to do something different, but I don't know what."

I invited her inside to chat and told her about my interest in old cemeteries. Her eyes lit up.

"Oh, I love old cemeteries," she said.

"Maybe we could create a course," I suggested. "We could slap a fancy name on it, like um . . . 'Cemetery Semiotics' or something." *What were they gonna do, fire me?* "We could do a field trip together and take our cameras."

"Great idea. I love it!"

Being more familiar with the region, Macky charted a tour covering nearly a dozen cemeteries in Northwestern Ohio. Our outing would prove to be my initiation into the statue stalking I would pursue for years to come. I walked around the whole day with my mouth hanging open, feeling as if I were on a treasure hunt or even a pilgrimage.

In West Liberty: We saw a woman chained to an enormous anchor; a woeful little supplicant atop a heap of stones, her features worn down by the elements, her mouth open in awe or agony in response to the German immigrant who lay dead beneath her; an angel holding a book and pointing to the sky.

In Piqua: a Classical angel with a black eye; a young woman flung over a headstone, distraught with weeping, her long hair cascading extravagantly in waves around her face—who says grief can't be beautiful? Another angel blowing a trumpet into the tree tops. Later, when perusing the AAA tour guide, I'd discover *Piqua* was Shawnee for "a man formed from the ashes"—a Phoenix, as I aspired to be.

In Fletcher: a woman clinging to a cross in the corner where a row of pines blocked the sun; two widows, or so I imagined them, seated atop ridiculously high pedestals, especially surprising for such a small cemetery, facing away from each other, surveying the grounds, looking quite pleased with themselves. Beneath one of them, I sat on a stone chair with ornate carving, crossed my legs and smiled for Macky's camera.

In Mt. Tabor, we walked in a rural churchyard, sparse with rectangular tablets of white lit bright by the sun like Jesus, overlooking a patchwork of fields.[13]

Looking at the Victorian angels I came across, the Feminist Scholar within me wanted to write them off as sentimental emblems of the nineteenth-century, reminiscent of Coventry Patmore's now infamous poem "The Angel of the House," often used to bludgeon middle-class women of the era into the submissive roles prescribed for the ideal wife and later critiqued by Virginia Woolf, who declared angelicide necessary for liberating the woman writer.

But that deconstruction did nothing to satisfy my Pilgrim self who, hungry for spiritual sustenance, saw instead the numinosity of the statues. And so I wrested the Angel back from the suffocating confines of Patmore's domesticity and restored Her to the genuine archetype. To the Pilgrim me, the angels—often muscular and powerful in demeanor and clothed in Classical attire—resumed their original roles as divine messengers and mediaries; muses or daemons; protectors and guides, promising to lead the way out of the purgatory in which I had found myself. Their wings called to mind not delicate naïfs, but the powerful Nike, Goddess of Victory. To walk among these angels was soothing and

uplifting, to think of women with wings an inspiration.

"Do you think our fixation on cemeteries means we're depressed?" I asked Macky, partly facetious.

"I have a tendency toward that," she admitted, in the deadpan expression typical of her.

I wasn't convinced that explained it for me. But I thought that our being middle-aged women in a patriarchal society might have something to do with it, that we were mourning not only the loss of our youth but also something we only vaguely sensed had been lost.

That afternoon with Macky, the sun had been bright, the sky that deep azure of the best autumn days, and the white marble of the statues so dazzling it hurt our eyes. After a day of staring at them through the lens of a camera, my retinas retained images like a strip of film. And that night, as I fell asleep, visions of women and angels flashed on the blank screen of my eyelids like epiphanies of light.

Are You a Taphophile?
(A Checklist of Traits for Self-Assessment)

Please check all that apply:

Do you . . .

    ☐ *pant, drool, or feel heart palpitations when driving by an old cemetery?*

    ☐ *visit a cemetery at least once a month for reasons other than mourning a loved one?*

    ☐ *feel at home in a cemetery?*

    ☐ *find tombstone statuary and/or epitaphs fascinating?*

    ☐ *have no fear of cemeteries (i.e., are not taphophobic)?*

    ☐ *feel deliriously happy while walking in a cemetery?*

    ☐ *obsessively photograph cemetery grounds, tombstones, mausaleums, and statuary?*

    ☐ *have a taste for the sublime, melancholic, or gothic?*

    ☐ *find yourself collecting cemetery and/or funereal memorabilia?*

    ☐ *tend to be an outsider or see yourself as such?*

If you checked 4 or more, **Congratulations!**
You are quite likely a taphophile and should consider joining the Association for Gravestone Studies.

Plucked Flowers

By plucking her petals, you do not gather the beauty of the flower.
~ Rabindranath Tagore

IN MY TREKS through cemeteries, I've seen many a stone angel holding a petal plucked from the flower of life between her fingers. Arm extended, she holds out the petal as if about to drop it, as if she could suspend death, hold that moment in between the plucking and the fall to earth, the decay into dirt. It is sad to see a flower spent; yet this is part of Nature's cycle. But to pluck a living thing out of its own time seems an act of desecration.

I'd been wondering about this enterprise of teaching literature—or perhaps I should say, teaching literary criticism. Invariably, in every class, at least one student would refer to literary analysis as "tearing it apart." "Are we going to tear the story apart now?" "I don't like tearing it apart." I used to resist this, thinking it was a reflection of their own resistance; they often feel the same alienation about exploring symbolism. The activity is foreign to many of them, beyond their experience or inclination. But I began to notice that such complaints were most often made by the creative students, especially writers. Now that I was writing creatively, I was beginning to think they may have had a point.

In the nineteenth century, people often referred to literary works as flowers. You can still see remnants of the metaphor in anthology headings: "The Flowering of New England Literature," "The Flowering of Women's Literature," and so on. Up until recent years, literature was believed to be infused with the spirit of transcendent powers—with a green fuse of its own. This was the history behind the title of my book, *The Green Letter*. Literary analysis—the plucking of these literary flowers—was born from the desire to make literary study seem more "scientific," an early twentieth-century preoccupation. And then it really clicked in after World War Two, when literary criticism truly became an enterprise, when scholars gradually took over what had once been the province of poets, after the world was blown apart. The School of Plucking took hold and has since become even more vehement. Literary scholars often take delight in plucking off the flower petals with a kind of sadistic glee not unlike that of little boys who pull the wings off flies. Did I really want to teach this skill?

Yet there's a difference between analytic plucking and interpretation. With the motive of appreciation, interpretation can deepen your understanding and bring the spirit to the surface, rather than sucking it out and desiccating the flower. Interpretation is necessary to add life to the words, to give them breath. And sometimes, to see how the flower is made, you need to look closely, to learn how to make your own flower bloom.

But there is a fine line between that and analytical plucking. What was the difference? I wasn't sure. It may have been my professorial duty—while I still had a job, anyway—to teach English majors how to pluck in different ways (there are different modes of plucking) should they end up in grad school to become professional pluckers. But odds were, very few would take that path. And so I was torn between my dubious duty and a higher thought—the desire to help them love literature as one would love a flower. To love as a whole, rather than as pieces of a puzzle with gaps.

And as I yearned to be a gardener in my own right, I could see that all these years of plucking had dulled my creative faculties. Plucking favors the left side of the brain, making one's thinking lopsided.

For my own sake, I no longer wanted to pluck flowers for a living.

PEOPLE, TOO, CAN be plucked to death. The many petals of personality can be pried apart. Years ago, in grad school, I had done that to myself, and I hadn't felt the same since. A lover suggested we explore our "sub-personalities" (the various roles one plays, archetypes and aspects of oneself), and so I did. I pried the petals apart, plucked 'em—already, I was an expert plucker—and found thirty-eight different sub-personalities—and some subs had subs! When I was finished plucking and laying out all the petals for examination—what *was* the point of it, anyway?—I noticed something was missing. I could still recall that day. It was the day when I looked out the bedroom window at the Echinacea flowers and I could feel the empty space in my chest. At the very center, something was gone. Not only my spirituality, annihilated by dissertational plucking, but my spirit itself.

All my life, I had felt something there. How to describe it? It was like the beating of my own heart—*I am-I am-I am*[14]—but it wasn't merely mechanical. It felt like the essence of my being, the animation of my spirit. My core, that was how I'd always thought of it. The center that held me together, integrating all. My life force. It had always comforted me to know it was there. To feel it. Rely on it. It kept me going. And then—just like that!—it was gone. And I missed it. It seems that some acts truly change us forever.

Even after the plucking, a body reader at a psychic fair told me that she could see a very strong flame in me, in that very spot.

"Really?"

"Oh yes! Like a big furnace. It's very high and steady."

But hearing this got me no closer to feeling it.

"Dissection of personality is no way to self-knowledge," Freud once said, according to Joni Mitchell, who added, "All you get out of it is literature, not peace of mind. It's a satisfying but dangerous way to learn about yourself." Whether pulling apart yourself or literature, dissecting is deadly.

I WAS ALSO admitting to myself that I had doubts about finishing my tenure book, *The Green Letter.*

"You don't want to do it," Carolyn said one day at lunch.

"But I signed a contract," I said.

"You should see the expression on your face," she said. "Every time you talk about that book, you screw your face up in disgust."

"I do?" And indeed, I did. I could feel my face puckering up as she spoke, as if I'd just bitten into a sour apple. She was right: I didn't want to do it. I wanted it *done*, but even if I had the energy—which it seemed I didn't—I didn't want to spend another minute of my life on it.

That flower had been plucked.

The Planter Grave

An old white marble gravestone caught my attention.
A planter grave, I dubbed it, the shape of which always put
me in mind of a small child's bed.

Around the circumference of a small oblong grave was
a border of stone a few inches high to enclose the flowers
and plants.

But now only weeds grew in the planter.
The headstone bore a carving of a hand, forefinger pointing
upward, heavenward, the words in the stone faint as a whisper.

A Legacy of Light

For Maryclaire, at last

I miss thee, my Mother! Thy image is still
the deepest impressed on my heart.
~ Eliza Cook

I WAS CHASING the afternoon light down I-75 on one of my cemetery hunts through Ohio, when I saw the sign for Sidney. Any interesting cemeteries there? I wondered. I was in search of angels and other statuary to photograph. But Sidney was eighteen miles farther south. Maybe another day.

I remembered the last time I visited Sidney. I had gone there to attend a memorial service for Maryclaire Stone, who had been killed in a car accident. She had been a very special student of mine, the one for whom I had lobbied to share the Outstanding Student Award in English with Nathan, the little misogynist the guys in our department had been so keen to honor. In some ways, she had also been my teacher. The very best students always are.

Because her daughter was only five when she died, Maryclaire's family had requested friends and acquaintances to record our reminiscences for the little girl to read when she was older. Remembering Emily's visits with her mother to my women's literature class, I was eager to participate. Yet when the time came to write, I found myself up against an unusual kind of writer's block. The writers were to take part in mothering Emily, and I wasn't sure I was up to the task. There were several things I wanted to say, but I didn't know exactly *how* to say them.

I tried to picture Emmy at twelve, or perhaps sixteen (at any age, she was sure to be precocious), reading through the memorials lovingly written and compiled so that she might extend her own memories of her mother, but I couldn't get the little five year old out of my mind. How to describe an adult to a child? An adult known for her rich complexity and subtle nuances, for her very adultness? For that is what I loved most about the Maryclaire I knew. Though I was spared the task of explaining the tragedy out of which no real sense could be made, I nevertheless felt its burden. Whether my block was exacerbated by my own grief, or the fact that I had never had children or even been around them much, or because I had had so little experience with losing people close to me, or by my apprehension that, as an English professor, I might be expected to produce an elegy comparable to Tennyson's, I cannot say. But I was keenly aware that Emily had suffered a loss that went so far beyond words, it seemed presumptuous to say anything. I was in awe of her loss. Next to that, any words I might offer seemed small and insignificant.

It was now nearly five years since her death. Emily had grown five years closer to reading the eulogies for her mother. With pictures of stone angels in my head, I drove back north on I-75 at sunset, ready at last to break through the barrier between the living and the dead.

I DUG OUT the file of Maryclaire's papers, saved out of sheer appreciation. Ah yes, here's my favorite, "Mothers and the Women Who Daughter Them," which includes intimate stories from her own mother, Claire, told during some "wine-soaked" evenings together. My own mother had never shared such personal stories with me; I sometimes wondered if she shared them with anyone. We had never had an intimate "wine-soaked" evening the likes of Claire and Maryclaire, a scene I could scarcely imagine for us and for which, I must confess, I felt not a little envy. Aside from the personal stories I occasionally found in published books and articles, it was in the papers and journals of mother-students that I got a glimpse into these private lives that appeared to be so different from my own. But I doubted their own daughters would ever read them.

Tucked away somewhere in a box innocuously labeled "English 275" or "Women's Studies 201," they would most likely be destroyed or tossed aside by loved ones as uninteresting, puerile exercises written merely for academic credit.

Was there a box of Maryclaire's masterful papers hiding in some corner in the attic of Emily's house? Probably. Her family was very proud of her winning the Outstanding Student in English Award. Will Emily read "Mothers and the Women Who Daughter Them?" Should I send it, to make sure? Or should I return Claire's story to her, to bequeath to Emily when appropriate? And if I do, will Claire feel betrayed? Betrayed *and* proud *and* moved all at the same time, in awe of her daughter's insight. For all I know, Maryclaire gave a copy of the paper to her mother years ago. But for Emily, there is no substitute for the intimate telling that would have continued across the kitchen table, had Maryclaire lived into her daughter's womanhood, when secrets might be shared. Only words on the page.

I SAW HER sauntering across the faculty parking lot in that easy-going way of hers. The sway of her short, round body added to the effect. It was a beautiful autumn day, and unaware of my presence, she was smiling to herself like she knew the simplest secret of the universe. She might have been amused by some little antic of Emily's at breakfast that morning or by some childish wisdom uttered by one of her grade school students the day before—she was student teaching now—or perhaps by her husband's parting words. Or by any number of things none of us will ever know. But I always liked to think that she was just enjoying the day, happy to be a part of it. I knew her well enough to know that she was capable of that. Upon catching her in that private moment, I thought to myself with pleasure, "There she is, just walking along, smiling for no particular reason, without a care in the world. That's just like her. I should be more like that."

"Hey, Girl," we would say in passing in the hall, a couple of white chicks playing cool and laughing at ourselves for it. "One of these days, we're gonna have that cup of coffee." I had always hoped that, once she graduated, Maryclaire and I would become friends. We were of like mind and about the same age. Apparently, even our taste in men was similar. After seeing Ben, she had asked with a sly grin, "Who was that good-looking guy standing at your door?" I remembered once telling Patricia Smiley that I had had a student or two I wanted for friends (Maryclaire in mind) and getting a raised eyebrow in response. Why did I think she'd relate? What Smiley didn't understand was that Maryclaire's friendship would have been a privilege, for she had achieved a level of personhood that few ever do. In fact, she was one of the best people I have ever known. And I had always wanted to know more about how she had become that person.

When I finally met the woman who had been her mother and looked into her face, I thought I had a clue. There was Claire, lovely and distinguished and gracious—even at the funeral of her daughter. It was obvious: *she knew*. She knew who her daughter was. She had treasured her for exactly the right reason and would feel her absence all the more because of it.

On her father's side, Maryclaire once told me, was the matrilineage of no less than Lucy Stone, the great abolitionist and feminist, the original "Stoner" who in refusing to take her husband's name had started a tradition. And even though she had become a mother—the usual breaking point—Maryclaire, too, kept the Stone name and this matrilineage intact for at least one more generation.

But beyond these tidbits, I had little knowledge of how she had acquired her personhood. All I knew is that, as a young woman, she had lived and worked on the East Coast. I knew that she had a love of words, an eloquence which seemed natural to her, and the love of detail which marked her talent as a creative writer. I knew that, despite her exasperation, she had a knack for handling the racist blow-hard in our African American lit class with incredible tact, for which I was grateful on more than one occasion, even if it did go over his head. I knew that she had discarded Catholicism long ago and that she was an habitual early riser (did she write in those quiet hours before dawn?). Yet she also liked to play. She had always wanted to be a contestant on *Jeopardy* and that summer before she died actually got to compete on the show, much to her delight. (I never did get to see the video.) And I knew that her solidity was grounded in experience that had yielded a quiet, unpretentious wisdom—something few of us can claim—a solidity not to be confused with an overly consistent personality, locked into being itself (a type I have always found rather boring) nor with inflexibility or stodgy maturity.

No, the thing about Maryclaire was her integrity. That was what set her apart from other brilliant students. In her, at the most fundamental level, everything came together, all of a piece: her supple intelligence, her compassion and wisdom, her humor, the grace she had inherited from her mother. It was this unique integrity that came through in everything she said and wrote, in the very ease of her articulation.

Looking back through the file, I saw that my immediate reaction to the news of her death was a tribute to what she had achieved. I felt bad for Maryclaire that her life had been cut short, but I felt even worse for those who would no longer be able to benefit from her presence in the world: her family, her friends and would-be friends like myself, the students who would never have her for a teacher, the readers who would never get the opportunity to read her work. How many knew of her aspiration to write?

THE SUMMER BEFORE the accident, Maryclaire had given me a short story of hers to read, entitled "Raissa." (Emmy, have you found it yet?) We pledged to meet for coffee at last, to discuss it. I was a little surprised. I knew she aspired to write, but I hadn't realized she had already started. I never had the opportunity to tell her how good I thought the piece was. We never did have that cup of coffee.

In the months between making the plan and her death, the story sat in my study collecting dust, along with some clippings and an extra copy of Julia Cameron's *The Artist's Way* I planned to give her. I didn't know if she really needed this book, but I had looked forward to giving it to her as a token of encouragement and, perhaps, as a pact with a sister writer. Now, I saw this more clearly—that I needed the encouragement as much as she. We would have made great workshop buddies; she would have been as great a help to me—greater, perhaps—as I to her. In those days, however, my energies had been directed primarily toward encouraging other writers and artists, typical of what Cameron refers to as shadow artists.

One day, soon after I had heard of her death, the things I had gathered for her caught my eye as I walked by their perch in the study.

The book sat on top. Seeing it gave me a peculiar sense of doom. To whom would I now bequeath *The Artist's Way*? The question haunted me for some time. The death of the book's intended recipient seemed like a bad omen. Why? It was only now, years later, that I finally understood. Giving the book to someone was my way of keeping my own aspiration simmering on the back burner, while I deferred the dream for myself; without someone to give it to, I feared the aspiration would die out. But until I began writing myself, the inspiration I wanted to give to others was limited. I was like a mother (my mother) who projects her own thwarted dreams onto her offspring. "Go," she tells them, "go live the dream that I never could." How could I have forgotten that you could be a mother and a writer, that you could do both?

I remembered that Maryclaire had already been collaborating with someone. One day, I had run into her and Emily on campus. "Emmy's written a book!" she proudly announced. "Show it to Kathleen, Emmy." I took the small, handmade book, fastened with ribbons, and turned the pages in amazement. Emily's crayon drawings were accompanied by words telling a simple story. "She had a little help," her mother told me, a twinkle in her eye.

As I wrote about her, I pondered her name, *Maryclaire*, named for her mother, but with a difference: Mary. Mother Mary, Creator, Nurturer. Mother of Emily, Mother of Words. *Claire*, Mother of Light, Clarity. Clair de Lune. Illuminata. The secrets of light, the greatest secret of the universe. Casting light on to sorrow. And Emily? I consult a tiny paperback on baby names, bought on impulse in the checkout line: *Emily*—Artistic.

IT WAS A beautiful autumn day. Butterflies were in the trunk of Maryclaire's car. Or rather chrysalises that would transform themselves into Monarchs. En route to her assigned class of third graders early in the morning, she was probably smiling as she anticipated her students' faces at seeing a room full of color on wings. A young man in a pick-up truck on the other side of the road looked away for just a second, fumbling for a cigarette or a tape on the seat next to him, intending no harm. And then the shock, head-on. Sometime later, the trunk unlocked and opened; a flutter of gold spilling out into the light of day. The simplest secret of the universe on wings for anyone to see.

Based on a somewhat fuzzy account of her death, that was what I had imagined. I thought it would make a lovely, transcendent ending to my memorial for Emily. But after seeking some clarification on the details, I discovered that my romantic imagination had been working overtime. The Monarch chrysalises had probably not been in her car at all, but already in the classroom. And even if they had been in the trunk, their fate might well have been as final as the driver's. But not wanting to think about that possibility, I persisted. I rationalized. Poetic license. Couldn't I just leave the original, prettier version as it was?

But the dishonesty made me uncomfortable. And then it forced me to think about Maryclaire and about writing. About Emily. It would have been a cheap trick, those golden butterflies winging off into the azure sky of autumn, rather like the papier-mâché butterfly wired onto Walt Whitman's finger in the bogus portrait of him as an old man, "Sage with Butterfly," a slick PR stunt. And what *about* Emily? No symbolic flight into transcendence could restore her loss. A stone angel would be more comforting.

And then I realized that, for all her gentleness and tact, Maryclaire never backed off from the complicated truth. She was unintimidated by the complexities of life as surely she would have been by those of death. That was the crucial aspect of her talent: she would write her way through it. And so would I. And so perhaps would Emily one day, with her legacy of light.

Transport

I RARELY SAW a funeral in Woodlawn. And on the occasion I did, I felt uncomfortable, as if I were intruding. But I liked to imagine a Victorian funeral there: a hearse leading a procession through the hungry mouth of the stone gate; horses and carriage alike plumed with feathers, usually black, sometimes white; the horses plodding slowly as if in sympathy, with a *clop-clop clop-clop,* perhaps weeping for us, as Homer had said, so pitiful in our humanness.

†††

The funeral marches of old New Orleans must have been something to see—and hear: eerie trumpets played by saints in flat caps and uniforms of wool and brass buttons, peeling a sound that strikes the very chords of a place in your soul you didn't want to go to. The birth of jazz.

Today, silence instead. In respect for the dead and those mourning the loss. The modern carriage a streamlined station wagon, black or steely gray, moving like a shark parting the waves of traffic, limos in the wake, flagged with purple crosses. Funeral passing: Stop the car.

Jaguar Hearse

Maude: Harold, *everyone* has the right to make an ass out of themselves. You just can't let the world judge you too much.
~ From *Harold & Maude*

"OH YES," MARK was saying, "*Harold & Maude*. Funny movie."

His office being across the hall, it was a neighborly habit of mine to stick my head in his doorway from time to time. That day I had mentioned that *Harold & Maude* was one of my favorite flicks of all time.

He laughed, thinking of the film, and then he caught himself. "But, well, it's pretty sophomoric, isn't it?" He smiled knowingly, expecting me to agree.

But I didn't agree. His comment took me off guard. And as usual when feeling blindsided, I didn't respond directly.

"It's a cult film," I said. "In Bloomington, at Bear's Place—one of those bars that has a film series?—they used to show it every fall. It was a tradition. It was fun."

And with that, I retreated as hastily as I could back to my side of the hall.

"Sophomoric." Read: beneath notice of academic, intellectual types. Read: unworthy of the attention of sophisticated people. "Sophomoric." The word burned in my ear.

Okay, so maybe Harold's suicidal theatrics are over the top. So, maybe the movie is a study in juvenile excess, adolescent angst, seventies idealism. Maybe the story is simple, the sight gags unsubtle, the point a little too obvious. But it is hilarious. And moving, which I think Mark must have forgotten. And, in its way, a classic. How sad not to be able to enjoy it because of sophistication.

Sophistication for the sake of sophistication. As if one can't like both sophisticated and unsophisticated things; as if one person can't hold within them a diverse range of things that fall at various points on the scale of sophistication. As if, as the purveyors of refined taste, we were all duty bound to rate everything on this scale in the first place. How weary I was of it, yet everywhere in this narrow little world of compartments and empty rhetoric, I saw people cloaking themselves in the mantle of sophistication. Could they no longer remember what it was like to revel in out-and-out silliness? Did every tickle or belly laugh have to be predicated on inside jokes that only the erudite could understand?

Sophisticate (v.)

1. To cause to become less natural, especially to make less naive and more worldly;

2. to make impure, adulterate.

Root: *Sophist.* Gloss: one skilled in elaborate and devious argumentation, from the Greek philosophers (circa fifth century, b.c.e.), known for their elaborate and specious rhetoric.

Prayer: Please, deliver me from ever again worrying about being "sophisticated enough." I'd rather be a natural woman.

I WAS NOT yet a taphophile when I first saw *Harold & Maude* back in the fall of 1981. Although I enjoyed Harold's eccentricity, it would be ten years before my immersion in the sophisticated milieu of Academe sent me to the cemetery as a reflection of my own alienation. It was Maude with her unadulterated *joie de vivre,* along with her imperative to be true to ourselves, that made the film one of my all-time favorites. I love the whimsical little touches in the film, such as Maude's odorifics machine and her gyno-sensuous sculpture. I love the playful humor and gentle lightheartedness of the film. I love that Harold is revived.

Before he meets Maude, Harold himself is a victim of sophistication in its most shallow and insidious form, represented by his mother and ostentatious surroundings. His fake suicides are designed to get her attention and give her feathers a ruffle. But driving a hearse and attending strangers' funerals suggest a deeper alienation, along with depression. Does Harold feel dead inside? Would he just as soon be dead? Does he *want* to die? That would be one way of escaping from Mother. Later, Harold understands his real problem: "I haven't lived." In order to do that, he has to free himself from the shackles and uptight values of high society. And the vivacious seventy-nine-year-old Maude is just the person to set him free.

Of course, Maude is sophisticated in her own deeper way. Not unlike Mark, she is well educated and worldly. She has lost loved ones and suffered greatly, having been in a concentration camp, but she doesn't let any of it deter her from enjoying life, having fun, and speaking her mind. Despite what she's endured, she is optimistic and life-loving. Anti-establishment, anti-war, pro-environment, she is a liberal nonconformist, willing to break any rules that impede her. She is funny, whimsical, spontaneous, and sensual. She is an artist in every way. She is earthy and authentic. Although she's of an older generation, she embodies the youth culture and values of the seventies. And she is adorable. Is it any wonder Harold falls for her?

That Harold turns the new Jaguar his mother got him into a sporty little hearse is one of my favorite gags of the film. As an actual hearse, it's utterly useless. It's also a symbol of deadly sophistication that carries Harold like a corpse. After Maude dies, Harold flings the jaguar hearse over a cliff and emerges playing the banjo Maude had given him—an instrument usually considered unsophisticated and folksy—as a life-affirming gesture of his new freedom. All of which emphasizes how deadening sophistication for its own sake can be.

I LIKED MARK, I really did. I even considered him a friend, to the extent one dare think of a colleague that way. I knew him to be a fine person. But sometimes someone says something that reveals a difference you're not sure you can bridge. In this case, what Mark said revealed him to be a hardened academic; that is, it exposed the academic core of his way of seeing the world. And increasingly, after my denial, this was the very mindset from which I was trying to free myself.

Mark would be one of the few colleagues I would stay in touch with after I left Beantown. But ultimately we would drift apart, as is typical of former colleagues, especially when one was denied tenure. Increasingly, it seemed, he took on the mantle of professorial propriety, whereas I continued to peel off its layers and, like Harold, liberate myself from its confinement.

Raven

NEAR DUSK, THEY light in branches—so many you might think you're in a Hitchcock film. So many Poe would've been overwhelmed with doom and nevermores. Bird by bird, they fly in for the convention at the big Catalpa, heeding the elder's caw. *Calling all crows. Tribal council in ten. Look sharp and be quick. Important business at hand.* By scores, perhaps a hundred, maybe more, the big black birds gather in the huge gnarly branches, hidden by leaves from groundlings doomed by gravity to inch their way along the cemetery path. *Alert: biped and quadruped at four o'clock, near Parmenter. Relocate. Repeat: relocate. Remove to Red Oak at McCorkle. Prepare for take-off. CAW. CAW. CAW.*

Suddenly the flock lifts off en masse, giving us what for. Startled and a little nervous, Mandy picks up her pace.

"Ah, poor Mandy, did the big bad crows scare ya?"

They startle me, too, but unlike my unamused sidekick, I think they're a hoot. I love the way they fly off in a sudden swoosh, the way they tell us off, so loud and raucous. And I know what they are saying: You made us move, but it is still our place. I understand their resentment. And I realize that, if they want to, they can cover us with their revenge.

There are lots of birds in Woodlawn, and I love them all. What would the cemetery be without the symphony of birds? But the crows—or ravens, if you prefer the more poetic appellation—add a necessary voice to the chorus, a tell-it-as-it-is, life-is-not-always-pretty-and-neither-is-death note of realism and even outrage.

And they are right: the cemetery is their place. The Audubon Society considers many Victorian cemeteries to be bird sanctuaries. Trees and birds go hand in hand. And what could be more fitting? Since ancient times, birds have represented the soul, the spirit. They are our angels, our messengers from heaven, our go-betweens. They are augurs and prophets. The soul in migration, the soul incarnate. The flight of fancy, imagination, intellect. The signature of God. The dream of liberation. On their deathbeds, the dying, it is said, see birds.

But the crows ground all this heady symbolism. Eaters of death, theirs is a carrion magic, a trickster's transformation, performed with angry insistence, indignation and sass. They are the loud, noisy ranters, kvetching and carrying on; yet they are also sleek soaring grace. Apollo's familiar, the Philosopher's Bird, the raven marries contradiction like a black cross in the sky, hanging on the wind, free from earthly consistency. They are the rightful overseers of the dead, the most appropriate conductors of souls on their journey.

What do I divine as I watch them in the sky, black letters on a big blue tablet? They speak to my own ragged soul, longing for flight. And I say to them: Yes, you are absolutely right. This is your place. A woman and her dog are only visitors here—at least until we, too, are buried in the earth and our winged spirits can soar through the universe as you do now.

Ici Repose

This is a critical moment in any story, an Ordeal in which
the hero must die or appear to so that she can be born again.
~ Christopher Vogler

FOR MONTHS, I'D been planning to take a self-portrait in
Woodlawn. It was to be in black and white, of course. The site: a small
grave on the hill behind the holding vault, featuring a monument
that looked like a baby's crib, with a border of stone meant to contain
flowers—now holding only weeds—and a headboard and footboard at
either end. In professor's guise, I was to lie in the bed, hands clasped over
my chest in repose. My attire: black velvet blazer, black pants, white shirt
and a narrow tie. Glasses, perhaps. Eyes closed or winking? Undecided.
Caption:

† HERE LIES...PROFESSOR DAVIES †

1992-1999

It was fun thinking about it. What epitaphs might I add?

Casualty of the Tenure Wars
Sudden Death on the Tenure Track
Murdered by Her Devious Fellows of Dubious Distinction
Death in an Untenured Position

Or perhaps I should go for something more elaborate and Mary Bakerish:

The Clock has Stopped,
The Mirror Covered;
Her torturous thinkings are o'er;
Her Breast Heaved
by Scholarly Affliction
No More.

I had had other ideas for self-portraits in cemeteries. À la Francesca Woodman: a blur of motion—slow shutter speed—making a ghost of myself. The shadow of an angel. Plaintive peering through the grille of a mauso door, hands clutching the bars; peeking pixie from around the side.

The problem was, I hadn't yet learned how to shoot self-portraits. I was unsure about whether the release cord was long enough. And as for playing the dead professor, a part of me wasn't comfortable with either lying on someone else's grave or being caught in the act. Wimp! And while I thought it was hysterical and apropos, yet another part of me inwardly shuddered at the self-deprecation it seemed to imply. Woodman's photographs were beautiful and ethereal in their way, but it was hard to look at them knowing she had committed suicide.

And then there was a practical challenge: the large rusty pipe arising from the center of the grave. I never had figured out what it was for, much less what to do about it so that I could lie on the grave without impaling myself.

So I had never taken the photo, and now I supposed I never would. Tomorrow, we were leaving Beantown for the Promised Land . . . Columbus.

COLUMBUS WAS NOT the most inspired choice. But nothing else had panned out. I had studied the "Best Places" lists and considered carefully when applying for jobs the previous fall. At one point, the Northwest had seemed attractive, Seattle and Portland cool and hip and home of grunge, which was something of a soundtrack during my years in Beantown. I applied for a job at a community college in Portland. But nothing came of it. Eh, just as well. Too rainy. And awfully far away from family and aging parents. And in general, moving across country with no job lined up was simply impractical. But nothing closer to home panned out either. One interview at a liberal arts college in Michigan had been particularly discouraging. The position focused primarily on teaching. But when I told the English department chair that I hoped, above all, to inspire students, he snarled, "Inspire them to do *what?*" Ugh. That moment was the last gasping breath of my attempts to find another tenure track position.

I had already decided I didn't want another position that focused on research like the job I had B.S.U.-Beantown. *Never again!* I wrote in my journals. *Never again* did I want to be held hostage by some project demanded of me by the system or to be subjected to the whims and scrutiny of that system and its members. *Never again* would I risk health and sanity for a job. *Never again* would I allow myself to be forced to live a workaholic lifestyle. I declared myself a free agent. Come what may.

To help you get in touch with your life's dreams and goals, it is suggested that you write your own obituary. In my imagined obit, the word *scholar* did not appear. Writer, yes. Teacher, yes. Spouse, friend, etc. etc. But not scholar. And so while it had been painful to let go of finishing my tenure book, in all practical terms, it didn't matter much ultimately, since I no longer wanted a job that demanded research. But since no one was offering that or any job for that matter, what I wanted was a moot point.

And so, with no prospects on my side, we relied on Ben to find the employment that would determine our next move. He landed a job in Columbus as a salesman for a wine distributor. Not likely a good fit, but it got us out of Beantown. According to the "Best Places to Live" list, Columbus had more overcast days than average. It did not make the top 100. Nevertheless, it was the default go-to city for Buckeyes. It seemed every person I knew from high school who hadn't stayed behind in Gallipolis moved to Columbus. Just because it seemed too obvious, too boring or even regressive, I had sworn I would never be one of them. But with nowhere else to go, Columbus-bound we were.

Briefly considering a new path, I met with a head hunter in Columbus to check out the options for someone with my qualifications. The best he could come up with was working at Victoria's Secret writing steamy ad copy for a bunch of sparsely clad anorexic babes. That didn't sound very appealing. I decided to stick with what I knew. Once we moved, I planned to collect unemployment for a couple of months while scoping out adjunct teaching positions, along with Victorian cemeteries in the area and beyond. At least Columbus was teeming with colleges and universities. Mandy had no definite plans other than to assist me on various cemetery outings.

I HAD ALREADY said my goodbyes to the folks on campus. Both Tim and Hyacinth offered to write strong recommendations for me in future job searches, as did the associate dean, who wholeheartedly believed in me. Likewise Ken Schmidt, but having seen a previous recommendation that damned me with faint praise ("Kathleen is a promising scholar"), I no longer wanted to use him as a reference.

Rather than live in Beantown, Mark and his wife, Malina, had opted to live in Columbus and commute, so Ben and I expected to see more of them. They had generously put us up when we hunted for a rental. While I packed up the office, other neighbors in Calvin Hall stopped by to exchange goodbyes and well-wishing. Di reassured me that she and Bruce would have many more parties they would invite us to and that they would visit us in Columbus. Cheryl, a colleague in education who left before I did, pledged to stay in touch, and she would keep to that promise.

When I visited Nan one last time at her home, I gave her a framed black-and-white portrait of the angel at the Beantown Methodist Church, where Ben and I got married.

"To watch over you," I told her.

She nodded, moved by the gesture.

I bent over her wheelchair to exchange a hug, or rather a semblance of one, with care not to crush her tiny, fragile body. Her kitties, Percy and Eliot, somewhat begrudgingly jumped off their perches on the chair to make room.

"I'm going to miss you, Nan," I said, tearing up.

"Who will I share all the gossip with now?" She laughed, trying to brush it off.

"We'll be in touch." But not as much as she would have liked, as it turned out.

Carolyn and I planned to reconnect in Columbus, since she would be there often to visit her son. Jack and I were in the middle of a tiff over the disappearance of *Born in Flames*, a movie I had loaned him. He angrily dumped books I'd loaned him off at the house, despite my wanting him to leave them on campus instead. I was pretty sure his behavior had more to do with being upset about my leaving than anything else. I wasn't sure whether we would remain in contact, but once we moved, the first letter I got was from him.

Although I had formed some attachment to it, I wasn't sure if I'd miss the frumpy little house on Hazel Avenue; moving to a much nicer, more modern rental on the cusp of the outer belt in Columbus was a relief. But much to my surprise, I was going to miss Beantown, where so many important life events had happened. And of course, I'd miss Woodlawn Cemetery most of all.

MANDY AND I went for one last walk and made our rounds to all our favorite sites. I bid farewell to the sphinxes, the "dearly departed" lady, the sad little lady with the wreath, the lady with open arms reaching up into the tree tops, the sailor and the soldier who stood watch over the veterans' memorial. She romped one last time in the ravine where she had chased many a squirrel and groundhog.

I thought about the comfort I'd felt walking there that first time nearly seven years before and throughout the struggles in the years that followed. The cemetery and all its positive symbolism taught me to value transcendence and to have faith in my own resilience. From the grave of "Professor Davies" a new me would emerge. I had no doubt that I had survived with my soul intact, and the knowledge strengthened me. But I couldn't help but wonder if I wasn't leaving a piece of my heart behind. The thought brought tears to my eyes.

And then I heard the carillon ring out from the cemetery office, as if to signal that our time there was done.

PART II

GATHERED HOME

Crossing the River

Cross over to the other side of Jordan,
No longer in the wilderness to wander.
And when you reach the other side,
you shall be free.

~ Lyrics from a Traditional Hymn

I WAS STUDYING the white zinc monument in Newark's Cedar
Hill Cemetery featuring a bas relief image of the deceased lying asleep in
a boat like Charon's barge being ferried over the River by an angel. It was
a lovely image, really, and a nice metaphor for the crossing over from life
into afterlife. And since, figuratively speaking, I had died on the tenure
track back in Beantown, I decided to adopt it for my own crossing over
to Columbus. After all, we had crossed the Olentangy River to get to our
new home in the suburbs and then down Stygler Road—or the River
Styx, as I called it—toward Gallery Street, where the house we were
renting was located. Given my circumstances, I couldn't decide whether
I had crossed over into Heaven or a higher level of Purgatory, but it was
a relief to be free from my former life. And like Aeneas, who is ferried
by Charon to the underworld, I was eager to see what destiny awaited
me on the other side.

I took special pleasure in the symbolism of living on Gallery Street.
After the move that summer, I got serious about photographing cemetery

statues and monuments, eventually taking a continuing ed class in darkroom technique—it was on Main Campus but I'd be damned if I'd let that deter me—and then later joining the newly opened Insight Studio (the mainstreaming of digital photography a few years away), which would lead to exhibiting my work. Was living on Gallery a sign of good things to come? I wanted to think so.

I began to see signs and synchronicities everywhere, or at least that's how I interpreted the meaningful coincidences that seemed to occur on a weekly basis. As I committed to writing the book, many books, quotes, and images relating to cemeteries started coming my way. When a used copy of Natalie Goldberg's *Writing Down the Bones* arrived in the mail, it contained a bookmark from a bookstore in Taos, New Mexico that featured a skeleton wearing a fedora, cigarette in hand and one bony shin casually crossing the other, cool as you please. I had to laugh. It reminded me of the Grateful Dead skeleton dancing on the window in my old apartment back in Bloomington my last year there, when this ongoing adventure began. Stumbling onto Terry Tempest Williams's *Leap* led me to a key concept for the development of the book: the Living Symbol, Jungian Gerald Adler's term for a powerful archetypal image that unexpectedly—often fatefully—enters our lives to reveal something meaningful and important that we need to consider. Ironically, the cemetery was my living symbol. Later, one of my adjunct gigs would have me teaching Virgil's *Aeneid*, which featured old Charon ferrying Aeneas across the Styx into the Underworld to discuss his destiny with his father.

Like angels bearing special messages, these and many other books and references would nudge my thinking forward and, by virtue of their synchronous appearance, inspire and encourage me to continue. It was like that famous quote attributed to Goethe, which also came my way during that time: " . . . the moment one definitely commits oneself, then Providence moves too . . . . A whole stream of events issues from the decision, raising in one's favor all manner of unforeseen incidents and meetings and material assistance, which no man could have dreamed would have come his way."

MEETING OTHER PEOPLE did not come so readily. When you move to a city in middle age without a job or school-age children to connect you to others in a natural way, this becomes more difficult. Those you do chance to meet tend to have an established group of friends and are therefore in little need of cultivating or including new ones into their social circle. Such was the case, too, for people I met at the Unitarian Church and meetings of the Democratic Socialists, though the latter had some great parties. Later, once I started teaching again, I would meet my sister-adjuncts, Amy and Sonja, who would become long-time friends. Eventually, too, I'd join a writers' group. But in the meantime, there were only a handful of friends there I already knew—Mark and Malina and another woman I knew from B.S.U.-Beantown, an old high school friend with whom I was no longer close, and a couple I knew from grad school days (she had also been denied tenure at B.S.U.).

A drawback to socializing with Mark and Malina was his tie to B.S.U.

"We're going to have a party, and you and Ben are invited," he said. "But I should warn you, Ken Schmidt will be there." Like Mark, Ken preferred to live in Columbus and endure the long commute, rather than live in Beantown.

"Oh," I replied. "I don't think I'd feel comfortable around him."

"I'm sorry, but I have to invite him." Mark didn't have tenure yet, so he had to stay in Ken's good graces.

"Yes, I understand." And I did. But as much as I wanted to go to the party and forge new connections, my drive to avoid Ken was stronger.

Needless to say, I wanted to avoid running into anyone from the English Department on Main Campus. Even though they offered adjuncts the highest wage, I made up my mind I would never apply there. Though I loved the Borders Bookstore in Columbus, it was located in the section of town where I knew many of my former colleagues lived, so after seeing one of them there once, I avoided it altogether, opting instead for a nearby Barnes & Noble, where I wouldn't have to be looking over my shoulder every second.

Although I had never thought I'd live in the burbs—definitely not a hip choice, especially where we ended up—I discovered its great advantage: It was unlikely any of my former colleagues lived there, and so I could co-exist with them in Columbus, and for the most part, forget they were there at all. As it turned out, with the exception of the fellow in Borders, whom I hardly knew anyway, I never would run into any of them.

And so our social life was meager, but Ben's job at the wine distributer provided us with some prime samples—leftovers from Rombauer and the like—opened for prospective customers to try. So we had a lovely little wine-tasting party to which we invited Mark and Malina and my high school friend and her partner. Mark proposed a toast: "Cheers to your new life here!" A short while later, Ben would leave the job— he wasn't cut out to drive home the sales—and ended up working in B.S.U.'s accounting department of all places. Ironic that, once again, we were relying on that university for sustenance. He would have his own challenges with his manager, who was prone to hiring people who went to her church. Favoritism seemed to be embedded in the political culture of the place.

A YEAR AND a half after the move to Gallery Street, I would buy a house at a yard sale. Or that's what I like to tell people. It's not much of an exaggeration. It came from the most spectacular synchronicity of all. The house happened to be located across "the Styx."

After discovering a beautiful neighborhood park called the Village Green, I aspired to find a house near it so Mandy and I could walk there regularly without the hassle of having to drive over. One Saturday, I took Mandy to the park for our walk earlier than usual. On the way, I noticed there was a moving sale at a house only two doors away from the park's entrance. I stopped to investigate.

"So, you're moving?" I asked the owner.

"Yes, we are."

"Does that also mean you're selling the house?"

"Yes. Are you interested?"

"Yes! Definitely."

What luck! We exchanged phone numbers, and within a couple of months, the contract was signed. I don't believe anyone else even looked at the house. It was meant to be ours. And my parents' gifts of early inheritance made it possible.

Not only was the house close to the park but the creek that ran through the park also ran behind the property, which meant no one lived behind us, making it more private. Having been born and raised in a river town, I've always felt more at home living near water. And the house was so spacious, there was room for a study, a man cave and a guest bedroom. Essentially, there were three living rooms, largely unfurnished until we could afford to buy some furniture. For the first time, we had the luxury of a two-car garage.

Finding a replacement for Woodlawn proved more challenging. I missed it terribly and had hoped to find a Victorian Garden Cemetery that would provide spiritual sustenance. The most comparable in Columbus was Green Lawn Cemetery. It had some interesting statues and monuments, a nice bridge, and several state champion trees. It was considered an arboretum as well as cemetery; the Audubon Society had even left brochures in the office listing all the species of birds seen on the grounds for birdwatchers to record sightings. But being located in the south of town, it wasn't terribly convenient. Worse, I didn't feel entirely safe there. I did see other walkers occasionally, some with baby strollers even, which made it seem more benign, but once vandalism made the news, I wanted to avoid the place. So while I appreciated Green Lawn, I never felt at home there the way I did in Woodlawn.

The role of cemeteries in my life was shifting. I no longer needed a special cemetery in the same way I did in Beantown. Now from my central location, I was more interested in extending my travels to shoot all the cemetery photographs I could. And now, for my book, I was reflecting on the Victorian Garden Cemetery as my living symbol.

In my heart, it was the Village Green, the neighborhood park, that I found to be most like Woodlawn. The serpentine path that ran parallel to the creek and through the woods reminded me of it. The park was Woodlawn's secular replacement. I felt extraordinarily blessed to live near this space and to be able to walk there every day. Just like in the early days in Woodlawn, every day I would say as we walked there, "Oh Mandy, we are so lucky to have this place."

Another stroke of luck led me to a description of my destiny. I found it in a book I happened to see on display at the local library. The book said I was to "take the unseen forces of spirit and give them creative form or manifestation . . . to fully and in detail express my experience of the numinous." It *fit*. It was astounding how much so. It sounded like the task I had set for myself, my ambition to write a book about the cemetery as my spiritual landscape, my soul garden. If the source seemed dubious, well so be it. I got what I needed from it: the encouragement to continue.

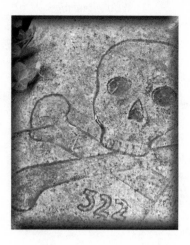

I ♥ Cemeteries

The bumper sticker in front of me read "I ♥ Cemeteries." Not the typical bumper sticker you see in Midwest suburbia, or anywhere else for that matter. I did a double take. Sure enough, the driver in front of me was bravely—no, defiantly—proclaiming to all the world that he or she loved cemeteries. I strained to capture a glimpse of the driver's face . . . without success.

I scanned the bumper for other clues of the driver's identity.

On the side opposite "I ♥ Cemeteries" was a menacing black and white image of a skull, logo of the Misfits, a punk-horror rock band. The driver was probably some goth kid. Not that I had anything against goths; in fact, they were usually among the most interesting students in my classes. But I guess I was hoping to see evidence of someone older, someone like me: more gothique than gothic, less inclined toward the dark and theatrical.

The light turned green, and we both got into the left turn lane. Maybe we'd end up at the same destination, and then I'd be able to see the driver's face. But no, apparently the self-proclaimed lover of cemeteries had banking to tend to. I briefly considered following but at the last minute yanked myself back from the brink of temporary insanity.

This is the closest I've ever come to being a stalker.

Romancing the Stone

Thou shalt not make unto thee any graven image . . . . Thou
shalt not bow down thyself to them, nor serve them.
~ The 4th Commandment, *Exodus* 20.4-5

SOMETIMES I THINK I'm an idolater. Probably every
photographer is. Photographing an image is like an act of worship. It's
not mere recording—not cool and detached—but intimate, motivated
by longing. It's pure romance, this wooing of the Beloved. One literally
kneels before the subject to take in its light. One bows down and serves.
"Photography is like a caress," Sally Mann says. "It's sanctification." To
photographers, the image is holy; we make it holy. God is in the eye of
the camera.

I WAS SHOOTING an angel in a Victorian cemetery in Lancaster,
Ohio, wondering why I was so obsessed with cemeteries and the stone
women who inhabit them. Was I still in mourning? Quite likely, I'd
never find another teaching position on par with the one I had at the
Twig. That *was* a loss. Funny, though, I still hadn't shed many tears over
it. Maybe I was in denial, repressing my grief. Maybe the sad stone ladies
mirrored my buried emotions. Maybe. I didn't find the theory all that
convincing.

I walked up to the statue to gauge the light bouncing off the stone, counting my steps along the way, then stepped backward to my original position . . . *one, two, three* . . . rechecked the focus, clicked the shutter. Immediately I started contemplating other shots. Near the angel were three obelisks, and I wanted to frame her with them, suggest that she was hemmed in by them. *That's what it's like for a woman in Academia*, I though, *being surrounded by phallic pillars of stone, obdurate and unyielding in their arrogance.* The truth was, when it came to my defunct career, I was more pissed than sad. Sometimes the cemetery photographs I took were an outlet for that, but I knew there were deeper reasons for my obsession.

Picking up from my tour with Macky of cemeteries near Beantown, Mandy and I followed through on my plan to cover any and all cemeteries within a ninety-mile radius, whatever was doable in a day trip: Columbus, Marion and Mansfield; Granville, Newark and Lancaster; Shadeville, Sunbury and Bellefontaine; various bergs along the way. I made elaborate preparations for my excursions. I took trips to the camera store to stock up on film, monitored the weather with the vigilance of a meteorologist, gathered maps when I could find them and charted intricate routes, made detailed checklists of all the photographic accoutrement and sustenance I would require. I had time on my hands. Until the calls for adjunct gigs came in, I took advantage of collecting unemployment. Thrilled to accompany me, Mandy was a stellar assistant, patiently waiting while I took shoots.

IN GRANVILLE, I found my Beatrice. I spotted her out of the corner of my eye when I was headed toward the gate, ready to give up on finding much of interest there. She was a small angel, standing under a large tree. Her wings were spread wide, and one of her arms held up a torch. I turned onto the path and got out of the car to get a closer look. She had a beautiful face, with blank eyes—no irises, as if the visions of this world were too much for her—and hair loose and wavy over her shoulders: Victorian Classical. But for all her appeal, I was dubious. What was this white, plasticky stuff she was made of? Some kind of resin, apparently. Twentieth-century Victorian Classical. Then I noticed the sun was kissing her face, and I decided to wait for the right shot.

I moved closer, first squatting, then sitting at her feet, cross-legged like a Buddhist in meditation. The light on her face flickered. Like the fingers of Orpheus, a mild breeze was plucking the branches of the tree to let the light pass through, but for only a split second at a time. I would have to be patient, not my forte. I held up the camera to frame and focus her, bracketing out the arm with the torch, cutting her off mid-wing to give fuller attention to her face, the camera weighing heavy on my arms. First shot, a close miss. The second also. I was trying to beat Orpheus at his game. Then, mercifully, he pulled that one certain branch aside so that the sun made a patch of light on her blind eye, and I snapped the shutter to capture the moment of her illumination.

In Mt. Calvary on the outskirts of Newark, I fell in love with an angel at the intersection of St. Michael and Our Lady of Redemption. She was nearly life size, crouching on top of a pedestal in an unusual pose, her face turned slightly at a beguiling angle. "Oh, I like *you*," I whispered, as I tried this angle and that. So many possibilities. "I could shoot an entire roll of film on you alone."

Earlier that day at Cedar Hill, the big cemetery in Newark proper, I photographed a lady in mourning. She was seated next to a mausoleum, facing one of its walls, and like so many of her sisters in grief, she was holding a wreath. The sun splashed light on the mauso wall, throwing her shadow in relief and, in fact, creating a halo around it. And there she sat in frozen grief, looking forever at that dark effigy of herself. "Facing the shadow," I said to Mandy, who cocked her head in that adorable canine way as if to say, *"Really?"* For the Shadow Lady's portrait, I stood just outside the wrought iron fence that fringed the edges of the plot like a ruffle of black lace.

And on and on—scores of women, hundreds of shots. I liked to shoot them up close and personal, zooming in on their faces. It was as if I couldn't get close enough, as if I were trying to get inside of them, become them. I couldn't get enough of these stone ladies. I had to have them all.

"You shoot so *many*," Ben said, looking over the prints when they came back from the shop. "You'd think you were a fashion photographer."

Oh yeah, I thought, *these girls are my models.* Robes and chitons never go out of style. They're like the Chanel suit or the little black dress of the Underworld. The look is usually staid and reserved, but occasionally, a chiton slips provocatively off a shoulder. *Look sexy, darling. That's right, show a little shoulder. Look demure for me, baby. Give me that pout. Look sad.*

"Now me, I like to take my time," he continued. "I might spend fifteen, twenty minutes to set up one shot."

It was his nature to instruct. I was using his camera, an old 35mm Nikon he'd picked up second-hand some years before, and he had taught me how to use it. But he didn't understand that this wasn't about taking the perfect photograph. It was about connecting to something— something sacred and soulful, it seemed to me, though I wasn't yet able to put it into words.

IF I HAD been raised Catholic or, better yet, Eastern Orthodox, I might have had a context for my mania. But I wasn't raised Catholic or Orthodox. I was raised Methodist in the dullest of churches (which was probably a blessing) where I was lucky to get stained glass windows to feed my hunger for images. And by this point, I didn't consider myself religious at all. The closest substitute I had for either church or sacred grove were the Victorian garden cemeteries I haunted, which I esteemed as a blend of both. I went there to pray and worship in the only way I knew how—by photographing statues of angels and women.

I might not have been Catholic, but that didn't stop me from slipping into Catholica, a Catholic book and gift shop I discovered in the neighboring burb. When I came home with a small sack full of laminated saint cards and other goodies to put on the nightstand by my side of the bed, Ben shook his head and rolled his eyes. "My wife's turning into a Catholic!" he cried, partly joking, partly in alarm (although he was raised fundamentalist, he now considered himself a deist). I wasn't "turning Catholic," of course—I was a confirmed heathen, after all, way beyond conversion to any religion—but I was hungry for images, especially those that hinted of the divine. And so, I felt strangely at home in Catholica.

For Catholics and Orthodox, icons are doorways into the sacred. They are mediators, conduits for channeling the divine. Looking at them with reverence is considered to be a form of prayer, and one's relationship with the icon figure is supposed to be a two-way exchange. "If a door is to do its job, it must have throughput in two directions," as Linette Martin explains it. Pay close attention to their faces and hands especially, she suggests, and you will find "rest for the soul." Without the benefit of instruction, context or tradition, this was, of course, precisely what I was doing. Well, if you can ignore the fact that most of my girls weren't exactly religious icons. It was as if I had tapped into what Jungians call the collective unconscious, or as if spiritual instinct or intuition, if there be such a thing, had guided me to stumble onto this spiritual practice.

This I would later understand with crystal clarity, but then, my understanding was swathed in a proverbial cloud of unknowing. All I had to go on were my own fuzzy inklings and a strong but possibly batty passion for taking photographs of cemetery statues. I had no one to talk to about it, much less the words with which to articulate or at least grope toward an articulation of what I was doing. And so, that winter, I did what many others do when they don't trust their own intuition, I consulted that secular priest of our time, a psychotherapist. That I would do such a thing was a measure of my confusion, for I had sworn off therapy and even "self-help" years before. At its roots, *Psyche* may mean soul, but the therapists I had hitherto encountered seemed poorly educated in the mysterious ways of that elusive faculty.

"I'VE BEEN PONDERING your fixation on angels," she said, a number of sessions in, "and I think I've figured out what it means." She smiled brightly; her eyes glistened. This was a moment therapists dream of: being the catalyst for a client's A-HA! moment.

"What did you have in mind?"

"It's their wings. They represent your desire to be free." She looked very pleased with herself.

This theory was but an extension of her master narrative of me. "I see someone who pushes herself down," she had said time and again, pressing her hand in a downward motion to illustrate how I suppressed myself. For weeks, I had watched her on the couch opposite mimicking my hunched-over self, and frankly, it was starting to grate on my nerves. And so, I'm afraid I wasn't very receptive to her interpretation.

"Maybe," I said, noncommittal. "I'll think about that." Yes, it seemed obvious: Angels have wings; wings symbolize flight and by extension freedom; ergo, angels represent a desire to be free. But wasn't it a little too obvious? I mean, wouldn't I have thought it myself? I had a Ph.D. in literature, for crissake.

She meant well, of course, and the angels did represent spiritual transcendence to me. The problem was, it wasn't only angels I was fixated on. All the stone women of the cemetery struck a cord in me; whether or not they had wings was beside the point. There was a strength and power in these women. Most were, well, statuesque and even muscular, in the Greek manner. They filled me with longing not so much for freedom as for contact with the divine. At the very least, I saw them as my muses, and maybe something more—deities or secret saints who spoke especially to women. I thought of Patti Smith's line: "I see her my muse jutting around round round round like a broken speeding statue." I imagined Patti herself whirling round round round on the stage like a dervish in ecstasy. I imagined her benediction for "Dancing Barefoot": *the promise that she is blessed among women.*

It was beginning to dawn on me that my girls were all the therapy I needed.

IN THE DARKROOM, miracles can occur; the alchemy of reversal and resurrection. A flash of light, and white turns to black, black to white, though still invisible to the human eye. Baptism in a bath of silver, and partial images appear: the tip of a wing, an eye turned upward toward the sky or down to the earth, ridges on the rough bark of trees, a column, a face, a flower slowly emerge . . . until at last She rolls away the stone from her white tomb like Lady Lazarus. With the magic of toning, another reversal. Bleach makes the image disappear: Now you see her, now you don't. Then a dunk in sulfuric sepia, pungent eggy smell: Now you see her again. Rinse and dry, mount and press; toxins down the drain. The return of spring, summer and fall.

In the darkroom, miracles can occur, but not necessarily. Divine intercession is needed, prayer and patience required. On a shelf above the trays, glowing in the dark, is a phosphorescent Mary, accompanied by a tiny cat, perfect familiar who can see in the dark—reminders that what you create is not yours alone. *Holy Image. Holy Imago.*

It was in the darkroom at Insight, appropriately enough, that I finally understood the purpose of my obsession. There is something about the process of making your own prints that reveals artistic intentions you weren't fully aware of when you snapped the shutter. Like the gradual emergence of images in their bath of silver, insights come to light slowly, conceptions tumble from their womb/tomb and into the light of day, solid and whole.

I knew that it was probably Barb, one of the founders of Insight, who had put Mary and her little cat on the shelf in the darkroom. That would be like her; she has a playful and ironic sense of humor. But I was unsure of how she felt toward the images I was producing. I sensed they made her uncomfortable, that she thought them too conventional and quaint and wondered what I was up to. Was she also apprehensive that I was an uptight Christian who would spoil the fun? God, I hoped not.

We stood together just outside the black curtains of the darkroom, looking at my girls as they came out of the dryer. I don't recall her voicing the question, but it hung in the air so palpably, I felt I had to answer it. I didn't know what I was going to say, until the words bubbled up from the depths and burst from my mouth.

"I'm exploring the sacred feminine," I told her. "That's what these statues represent to me."

"Oh, I see," she said. And then she looked me in the eye and smiled.

IN THE BEGINNING was the image[15]. Not the Word, but figures of voluptuous women, goddesses who were worshipped and revered. This was the time before patriarchy, before the alphabet and the written word, before the Holy Word and the Word Incarnate. In the beginning, images fed people's souls.

It made sense to me that my obsession with the statues began at a time in my life when I was tired of words. I had spent nearly a decade doing little else but read, teach and write about literary "texts," as we called them, in a profession that had come to belittle the restorative power of words and anything else that hinted of spirituality or transcendence. It was understandable that, being word weary, I turned to images instead and, too, that I longed for something that would validate women and venerate feminine ways. But what astounded me was how the two came together, how like some latent prehistoric urge, my own blind desire—along with what? amazing grace that could save a wretch like me?—propelled me onto a path that people had traveled thousands of years ago. Those statues were my goddesses. After being an exile in guyville for so long, Goddess knew I needed them.[16]

Little Bastiani

WHEN I WAS a child, I used to accompany my parents to Mound Hill Cemetery when they tended my paternal grandparents' graves. Inevitably, I would grow restless and wander off to explore the neighboring headstones.

A few plots over was my favorite, the Bastiani memorial featuring a cherub and an oval black-and-white photograph of a young boy mounted on porcelain. He was a beautiful child of Italian descent with black hair and enormous deep-set eyes, and he was dressed in a little jacket and knickers of black velvet, with a big bow tied around his neck. His name was Oscar, after his father, and I was enthralled by him.

"What happened to him?" I called to my father the first time I saw him.

"He drowned in the river," he replied, "diving off the ice breakers."

The Ohio River flows by my hometown of Gallipolis. Meant to break up ice for docking boats, the three enormous blocks of concrete look like giant ice cubes. In the water surrounding them, the undertow is said to be particularly dangerous. I tried to picture Oscar jumping off the piers, laughing with his friends, then flailing in the water.

"Don't ever do that," Dad added.

I'm not sure why I was so fascinated by Little Bastiani. Perhaps because I was about the same age as he when I first saw his portrait and something in me related to the buried child. Knowing the living members of his family added to his mystique—his brother, the rotund Panzo, who had inherited the secret recipe for the best spaghetti sauce I'd ever tasted, served at Oscar's, one of the nicer restaurants in town; and Panzo's beautiful, olive-skinned daughters, all several years ahead of me in school. Whatever the reason for my enthrallment, I never grew tired of looking at his portrait.

The last time I looked for little Bastiani's portrait, I was heartbroken to find it missing, probably ravaged by vandals or the vandal of time.

The Buried Child

The original, shimmering self gets buried so deep
that most of us end up hardly living out of it at all.
~ Frederick Buechner, *Telling Secrets*

The language of depressed women reflects the experience
of inner division and appears in repeated references to a "real
self" that is not allowed expression, in the language of "burying"
and "hiding" the real self.
~ Dana Crowley Jack, *Silencing the Self*

SOON AFTER WE moved to Columbus, I took a pack of cigarettes, a pen and a legal pad out to the garage with me and began writing. At the top of the page, I wrote, *The Buried Child.* The words bubbled up from the depths. A voice in my head urged me to continue: *Write about it. Write your way through it.* And so I did, the words pouring out, page after page.

I instantly recognized the buried child as myself, or rather a younger version of myself. I had seen her in the childhood photographs I had been going through. Aside from a couple of baby pictures, most were square black and white snapshots with scalloped edges, taken with the old Brownie Mom and Dad used to have.

One in particular haunted me. In it, the four-year-old me is standing on tip-toe in front of a swing in the backyard, wearing a zippered seersucker sun suit that emphasized how short-waisted I was. I am hunched over and tentative in my expression, a shrinking violet if there ever was one, looking like I want to disappear. I try to smile for the camera like I'm supposed to, but I don't feel cute at all, and with the blunt bob of my dark hair, bangs exposing far too much forehead, I'm not. My God, what *were* they thinking? I look lost, as if I haven't a clue in the world about who I am. I look as if I find life challenging, though except for an overprotective mother and the bratty playmate half-visible in the photo, I didn't know why I might have felt that way.

It wasn't as if I'd had horrible, terrible parents. My father was emotionally distant but hardly negligent by any stretch, merely quiet and bent on succeeding as a businessman and being the consummate provider. My mother, the worrywart, was rather intrusive—I'd come to think of her as the body police—but well-meaning. Born six years ahead of me, my brother had successfully defended his claim to being the center of attention, which marginalized me to some extent. (Had I felt obliged to downplay myself to "make room for Danny"?) This arrangement also led to pigeonholing us: He was "the outgoing one"; I was "the shy one."

Still, my mother often told me how badly they'd wanted a little girl, and I could remember no incident of abuse or meanness that would explain the deep sadness I saw in the eyes of the timid little girl in the snapshot.

Had I always been that way? I got out my baby pictures to compare. Nope, no sign of being depressed or withdrawn. In fact, smiling effortlessly into the camera, Baby Me looked downright ebullient: *Hello world, here I am! Happy to be here.* And in an instant I knew: *This was the real me, this exuberance my native temperament.* I looked back and forth between the baby portrait and snapshots of the four year old. *How did I get from this to that? from the ebullient babe to the incredible shrinking girl?*

I considered the photographer's mirroring influence on my demeanor—Mom's especially, as she exhorted, *Stand up straight! Throw your shoulders back!*, exhibiting how it is done in exaggerated form (*so annoying*), not realizing I shared the same condition of scoliosis she had, indeed not yet realizing she had the condition herself—only one of many unwelcome inheritances from the female line. Was I merely reflecting her disapproval? Or perhaps she projected the self-loathing many women feel about themselves onto me, as a miniature version of herself, and I absorbed it like a sponge. Or maybe I absorbed her anxiety and self-doubt.

And what about Dad? I recalled a two-by-three-inch snapshot of Dad holding me as an infant in front of the house, wearing a suit and a fedora—a businessman's duds—and something like a smile. What mattered most was simply that he was holding me—that I had solid proof that he had ever done so—for good, gentle fellow that he was, he could not even hug, much less hold me now, nor had he for as long as I could remember. Nor did he tell me that he loved me. But then, he didn't tell my brother or his grandkids that either. I assume he said the words to Mom, though she once told me he wasn't a hugger.

All I remembered was adoring my dad and wanting his attention. And certainly I got it on occasion. I remembered him carving figures for me in Ivory soap and the gifts he brought back for me from buying trips for his jewelry store, the miniature salt and pepper shakers from the airlines for the dollhouse I'd made from a cardboard box and the stuffed version of Manfred, the blue dog from *Tom Terrific* whose eventual disappearance left me heartbroken for months afterward. Maybe other factors contributed to feeling overlooked by him. When I was four, the store caught fire. His father died as well. It must have been a rough year. He was too stoic to ever betray stress or grief, but it's quite possible I picked up on something, took it personally, felt neglected, through no fault of his own. Who knew?

I came up with various theories for who installed the dimmer switch on my beaming baby self, for how it happened and why, but the truth was beyond my grasp. All I knew was that I had a life-long habit of self-deprecation and that this had caused me grief time and again, especially in Academe.

WHAT HAPPENED LATER, starting with adolescence, was clearer. Even at forty-four, I was still hearing the same remarks I'd heard as a teenager. *You're spoiled. We should've spanked you more often as a child.* For decades, "You're spoiled" had puzzled and maddened me, leaving me with a vague sense of guilt and worry. *Did my parents think I was ungrateful for all they'd given me? that I wasn't aware of how lucky I'd been to have them for parents? What had I ever done that would make them think that?* During a visit home, I finally saw through it.

My mother showed me the childhood snapshots of my brother she'd gathered for his fiftieth birthday. She'd amassed quite a few, which is what inspired me to get out my own. Little Danny in his cowboy suit. Little Danny tap dancing. Little Danny with the fish he caught. In his bow tie and crew cut. With his friends surrounding him on his twelfth birthday. All the many pictures of my brother as a child.

"Wasn't he darling?" she said, her eyes lit up with adoration as she showed them to me.

"He was cute," I admitted. "How come you have so many more photographs of him than of me?"

"Oh, that's just because he was the first born," she replied.

Apparently, photographing the first kid like crazy kills the thrill.

The Danny stories followed next. How, for payback after being spanked—never brutally by any stretch of the imagination—he'd run to the window and yell for all the neighbors to hear: *THEY'RE BEATING ME! THEY'RE BREAKING MY ARM!!* Hahaha. Or the all-time favorite: How he broke into the miniature antique safe in Dad's closet and, not knowing the value, stole his collection of Indian head pennies to buy bubble gum and candy at the Crumpet Hut around the corner. Haha. Stories of how bratty he was as a child repeated with never waning enthusiasm.

"You know, I find it interesting that I was the good kid, yet there are no cute stories about me. Guess I should've been a brat." I hoped the humor softened the snark in my voice.

"You were good," Mom replied, "until you turned thirteen. Then you turned into a brat!"

"But there aren't any cute stories about that, are there?" I challenged, the snark coming through. "Besides, maybe I needed to assert my identity after being compliant for so long. That's what thirteen year olds are supposed to do, after all."

And then came the teasing derisions:

"Ah, poor little thing, you were *so* mistreated."

Dad corroborated: *You're spoiled . . . .*

To which Mom added, *We should've spanked you more often.*

Once I whiffed the stench of manipulation, I began to notice that merely speaking my mind was enough to trigger a "You're spoiled." This was especially true with my dad. It was as if demonstrating loyalty and gratitude to my parents required sharing their every belief and value. If I didn't conform to them, I was "spoiled." It really didn't have anything to do with gratitude at all.

This was an epiphany. Being "spoiled" was a shorthand way of expressing a litany of criticisms. It meant being too liberal minded, too intense, too sensitive, too honest and unwilling to conform. Being "spoiled" (or "sporled," as my dad pronounced it, as if struggling to get the word out) meant being *different.* How twisted was that? It was a double whammy, guaranteed to put me in a head-lock for life: Not only was I relegated to the margins, but my very identity was beyond the pale of the family values—I was the weird one, the odd duck, the black sheep, or so I sometimes felt. Only my academic accomplishments saved me. I was the shy one and the weird one, but also the smart one.

As a result, I didn't feel loved for who I was, but in spite of who I was. And while it may be somewhat commendable to love someone despite their perceived flaws, not being accepted for who you are still hurts.

In the car on the way home, Ben shared his observations of the family dynamics at the dinner table. "Your dad and brother definitely dominate the conversation," he said. "All they want to talk about is business. And you're right, you get interrupted a lot. Now I understand why you're so sensitive about it." It was true. To get a word in edgewise, I always felt I had to talk really really fast, which only made people less inclined to listen.

"Sometimes I really do think he's their favorite," I continued. Both of us being last-borns, Ben and I discussed sibling rivalry on a routine basis.

"Well, I think that's obvious," Ben said. Put so baldly, this stung a little. Still, I believed it was true.

"The irony is, Mom and Dad have always made such a point of *not* playing favorites." This, of course, was the keynote of their parental ethics. They scrupulously divvied up everything equally and never admitted they might prefer one child over the other.

"Maybe there's a reason to make a point of it," Ben replied.

"That's what I'm beginning to think, that it's a ruse—meant to spare feelings, but a ruse nonetheless. And why shouldn't he be their favorite? He's so much more like them. He shares their values, their politics. They have the family business in common. Even golf. It makes sense."

"Well, and don't forget, he's a male. I think that has a lot to do with it."

"Yes, of course—the gender factor," I murmured. I was remembering all the times Mom had told me how much they had wanted a girl. I had always found reassurance and comfort in that. But now, I was feeling skeptical. How easy was it to want a daughter, once they had already had their son?

But none of this quite explained the demeanor of that four-year-old girl in the snapshot, the well-behaved child who rarely ever did anything to earn a spanking.

I WISHED I found the little four year old endearing, but I didn't. I identified with the baby me, but not the other, the one who looked so lost, the one whose face and posture bespoke some obscure pain of my childhood. She didn't feel good enough, I supposed. Did her parents really love her? She wasn't sure. Maybe she was unlovable. That was the message she'd received, even though my parents had not intended it, even though I had no memory of what happened to make her believe they felt that way. I felt sorry for her and angry on her behalf, but strangely distant from her. No tears for the girl I once was were forthcoming. That in itself was disconcerting. I wanted to push the photograph aside. What could I do for her now?

I pictured an imaginary trip to Woodlawn, where this little girl and I placed wildflowers on her grave overlooking the pond in the back of the cemetery. Her being in two places at once didn't quite make sense, but I didn't question it. The past was past; that was what I needed to accept. I put the legal pad, along with some notes, in a large file folder and tossed it into a corner of my study, not wanting to look at it again any time soon.

A few months later, when I started therapy to help me cope with the loss of tenure, the little girl in the snapshot and my reaction to her came up again.

"You need to mother her yourself, give her the nurturance you feel she didn't get," the therapist suggested. "Try visualizing yourself holding her. Take some time each day to do it." For a while I tried it, and it seemed to help. But then I sloughed off, eventually stopping altogether.

Dear Virgil,

I am stuck here in the darkness, ghosts all around, and I have never felt lower or more lost. This is supposed to be a hero's journey—descent and triumphant return, a narrative of progress to inspire others. But I am no hero, and my life is not a myth. I am just an ordinary woman trying to find her way out. I am forty-four years old, and I've been wandering in the dark for a while now, and as much as I want this phase of my life to be over, it just isn't happening. There have been glimpses of light here and there, but overall, I feel stuck in a winter more overcast than usual.

I have been reading Richard Lewis, the jester of the Underworld. Humor helps when there is nothing else. His title says it all: *The Other Great Depression: How I'm Overcoming on a Daily Basis at Least a Million Addictions and Dysfunctions and Finding a Spiritual (Sometimes) Life*. He tells the story of his life as a basement dweller, sucking on a bottle, drowning in the waters of oblivion. His whole life had been one long "magical misery tour," a "wreck in progress." He admits that humility was what he needed. But humility is not what I need.

Thinking I should be over this by now, I tried therapy for the third time in my life, and as usual, it was a wash out. Therapists do not good muses make. I am looking for a woman carrying three lilies with stars in her hair counting seven. I am looking for a guide who can lead me out of here.

Yes, I know, it's easy to descend, far harder to climb back up into the light of day. Yet I know there's no point in ignoring these feelings, that it can be dangerous to do so. That one cannot force ascent; I've tried that before.

Virgil, this is my trip to the Underworld, the story of what I learned there, the questions that remain. Is it right to tell what I have heard? Is it right—and fitting—that I describe that deep world sunk in darkness? Is there a golden bough for me? Do you assist wandering women?

Angel of Melancholy

Melancholy can be overcome only by melancholy.
~ Robert Burton, *The Anatomy of Melancholy*

I DISCOVERED HER in Green Lawn: a melancholy little angel in bas relief, broken off from a gravestone and propped up against it. Wearing nothing but a skullcap, she was leaning on a tall, narrow trumpet as if in contemplation, a pose reminiscent of Antonio Canova's sculpture of the sad angel guarding the Stuart monument in St. Peter's Basilica. The trumpet reminded me of Gabriel, Archangel of the Annunciation: the message bearer. And like many images of Gabriel—and the Greek messenger god, Hermes, as well—she appeared androgynous (the drape overtop her trumpet obscured the front of her body), which reminded me of Virginia Woolf's insistence in *A Room of One's Own* that the mind of the writer of genius should be androgynous, with equal parts male and female. If grief was a woman, melancholy belonged to neither gender.

Regardless of gender, she moved me and filled me with longing. I connected with her somehow and took her into my heart. Through her, I understood that melancholia was important to contemplate and embrace.

WAS I DEPRESSED? Since I was denied tenure, I had often wondered.

The psychiatrist I consulted before we left Beantown had said my jokey self didn't seem depressed at all. My family doctor here in Columbus prescribed a minimal dose of Prozac, but it had no effect, so I quit taking it. Yet I continued to feel tired, my mood deflated. I felt alternately sad and anxious, occasionally irritable. After all, I didn't yet have a full-time job, and it didn't help that things were rocky with Ben, who was often prickly from the stress of being a salesman working on commission.

But was I *clinically* depressed? I exhibited none of the other classic symptoms. I did not weep for no apparent reason, or at all, for that matter. I did not have suicidal thoughts. I had not lost interest in hobbies or other activities that I had previously enjoyed. Despite my ongoing fatigue, I seemed to have an endless supply of energy and motivation to read anything related to cemeteries, death and the like, along with Rilke and various other books for inspiration; to visit cemeteries and take photos of statues and other monuments; to write about the cemetery and my life in Beantown. Misery had become my muse. And despite the gloomy subject matter, immersing myself in it made me feel not worse but *better*. How did that work?

One day I heard my mother-in-law, Janet, discussing temperament types.

"Keith's a choleric," she said, referring to Ben's brother and his tendency to lose his temper while playing board games with the family. He was a hot head and, among other more positive traits, tended to dominate others.

"Choleric?" I asked, nudging her to say more.

"Yes, one of the four temperaments. The others are sanguine, phlegmatic, and melancholic. I'm a sanguine." True enough. Janet tended to be upbeat, optimistic, and fun.

"Ben is a mix of melancholy and phlegmatic." True also. At times he could be gloomy, yet at other times unemotional, almost neutral toward others.

"I'm also sanguine sometimes!" Ben chimed in.

"Yes," I agreed. "Your little kid side—your cute side—is sanguine. But you're more Eeyore than Tigger, as you yourself have pointed out."

Since Janet was a fundamentalist Christian, I was surprised she had adopted this typology. Wasn't it a bit like astrology? I couldn't help thinking. Like astrology, humor theory was a handy tool for describing and understanding personality types. Fundamentalists see astrology as occult, a tool of the Devil, so it's off limits. But of course, humor theory wasn't quite like astrology. It had been around for centuries, going back to the ancient Greeks, and then revived during the Renaissance, when Robert Burton published his mighty tome, *The Anatomy of Melancholy*. Although the scientific basis for the theory—that personality type results from the predominant "humor" or substance in one's system—blood, black bile, yellow bile, phlegm—was debunked long ago, the fascination has held up because of its usefulness for understanding people.

"I'd say I have a strong melancholy streak," I said. "With a good dash of sanguine thrown in." I wasn't feeling especially sanguine these days, but I still believed it was in me. Nevertheless, I was beginning to look at my melancholy streak in a more positive way.

Those with a melancholy nature tend to be analytical and artistic. Having an eye for detail, they tend to be perfectionistic and critical. They are introverts who are deeply moved by beauty, especially the sublime. They are often sensitive and tenacious, inquisitive and idealistic. And so it is not surprising that many scholars and intellectuals—most notably theologians, which I always found intriguing—have the melancholic temperament. True, they can also be whiney and neurotic (*who, me?*), but I liked identifying with this group and found it comforting to count myself among them.

The melancholy traits fit me far better than the symptoms of depression. That's partly because they describe personality rather than malady. Melancholia is not a disease or disorder. It is not debilitating as depression can sometimes be. Nor does it lead to self-destructive behavior. One of its most important differences from depression is that it involves reflection, which helps us to distance ourselves from our past and other objects of our reflection in a useful way. It can also be pleasurable. This is why some call it an aesthetic emotion.

The reflection and distancing effect explained why immersing myself in my melancholy actually helped me feel better instead of worse. By embracing my melancholy side and converting it into art, I discovered a way out of the worthless self-absorption caused by my failure at B.S.U. Some people assume that memoirists are self-indulgent, but the process of writing about your life for others and focusing on the craft of writing actually takes you out of yourself and your life and what you've gone through. In contrast to writing in a journal for only oneself, that other-orientation is what makes it healing.

Jung once said, "Please remember, it is what you are that heals, not what you know." Exploring melancholia helped me to better understand and accept what I was, which I needed to do as part of my recovery after losing tenure. Melancholy was the cure for what ailed me. By immersing myself in melancholic topics—what could be more melancholy than a cemetery?—and making something from it, I had found a homeopathic cure. That was the Angel of Melancholy's message and gift to me.

Cemetery with a View

I GREW UP in a town with a cemetery on a hill. A hill so steep it requires a downshift to second gear. Sometimes when I go home to Gallipolis, I drive up to Mound Hill to take in the view. Like many locals and natives, my first impulse is to squint at the tiny town below and try to pick out the house I lived in growing up. It is obscured by tree tops, so first I have to find landmarks—the steeple of the Presbyterian church and the public swimming pool, built in the late thirties by the WPA, now drained from disuse—both close to my parents' home of over fifty years.

That settled, I look to my right, where I see the Ohio River winding its way alongside the town and beyond. It looks like a giant snake of brown or silver or even green, depending on the mood of the sky reflecting from above. I can see the three ice breakers Little Oscar Bastiani dove from, causing him to drown. On a clear day, I can see five miles upstream to the Silver Memorial Bridge, which commemorates the forty-six lives lost when the original collapsed in 1967. These are memento mori. As is the monument down in the park near the waterfront that features a rocker arm from the steamboat that brought yellow fever into the area in 1878, leaving sixty dead in its wake—one of the most peculiar monuments I've ever seen.

But the view of the river is so much more than a reminder of death. It's a way of seeing time all at once. Like a snake shedding its skin, the water follows the instinctive urge of the current, and the past feeds in, hitching a ride, gathering itself and flowing into the future, all the while returning to its Source. It is all One: The great unity of life and death. And on the other side? Almost heaven, West Virginia.

This is the cemetery of my childhood, my first cemetery, and it has profoundly influenced my ideas about cemeteries. Buried in my subconscious is the notion that cemeteries have less to do with submersion than with elevation, that cemeteries lift us up beyond normal sight to loftier perspective and insight. And because technically, the lookout site is called Fortification Hill, I have long thought of cemeteries as "fortifying." Never mind that Fortification Hill was originally established during the Civil War, complete with cannons. I'll take my fortification wherever I can find it.

A Graveside Chat

SARA PARRY DAVIES
1892 ★ 1963

I STOOD BEFORE my grandmother's grave remembering it was here, on a cold winter's day nearly thirty years ago, that I first sought comfort in a cemetery. I was only twenty, still living in Gallipolis, desperately pleading for marital advice.

"Dee Dee," I had said, hoping the nickname would magically invoke her presence, "what should I do? Please, tell me what to do."

I didn't know who else to turn to. My first husband, Richard, had been unfaithful, but my parents had disapproved of my marriage, so I couldn't admit to them I'd made such a dreadful mistake. My friends were away at college, but even if they hadn't been, I wouldn't have fessed up to them either. And so, in my secret desperation, I had somehow made my way to the cemetery on the hill to talk to a woman who promised absolute discretion and detachment. I listened intently in the stillness surrounding my grandparents' snow-blanketed plot, my ear pressed figuratively to her grave, waiting for Dee Dee to dispense wisdom.

When I was little, Dee Dee had dispensed her wisdom with great subtlety. I was painfully shy, "bashful," as my Aunt Helen always said when she swooped in for a hug, and I didn't have many friends, only a couple of bratty tomboy neighbors, the playmates from hell. One day, Dee Dee gently nudged me outdoors to play with Bonnie, whose mother rented one of the tiny houses on my grandparents' lot. From Dee Dee's kitchen window, we watched Bonnie sing to her dolls in the backyard. "Doesn't she seem like a nice little girl?" Dee Dee said. "She likes dolls, too. Wouldn't you like to join her?" *Uh-huh.*

Dee Dee was the only grandparent I remembered clearly. All the others had died by the time I was four, but I had Dee Dee until I was eight. I was her youngest grandchild and probably not her favorite—that honor went to my cousin Becky, the first grandchild, who had cristened her "Dee Dee" in the first place—but I was the one who most resembled her. This made me feel privileged, as if resemblance conferred special claim or connection. In her own wedding portrait, taken when she was twenty-four, she bore an uncanny likeness to me, or so I imagined. The brown toning of the old photograph accentuated her dark eyes and hair, turned her fair skin olive like mine.

But in all other respects, we seemed little alike. Dee Dee was the one most talked about at family gatherings, the one who inspired fond recollection and praise. She was the nourisher, famous in the family for her rich, cream-laden recipes—the ambrosia-like "Davies Salad" and oyster stuffing still reproduced by my mother and Aunt Helen for holiday dinners. Although a gentler one than most, she was the matriarch of our family, remembered for her Welshy shrewdness and for being adept at conveying her will with scarcely a word.

In contrast, I felt like a weak, sniveling mess. My husband had cheated on me with a sixteen-year-old girl, a cashier at the small supermarket he managed, who bragged about it to her high school friends. What could be more devastating? Not to mention humiliating. After Richard confessed, I wept for days. At first, he seemed remorseful, but after so much of it, he'd had enough. "It's like a damned morgue around here," I remember him sniping. And it was; something had died. There seemed no end to the weeping. But I believed in marriage and took my vows seriously, even if Richard didn't. And I couldn't bear for friends and family to know I had failed.

"Dee Dee, should I leave him? What would *you* do?"

I had thought Dee Dee was the perfect candidate for being my marriage counselor. According to my father, who got misty whenever discussing his beloved mother, her marriage was trouble free. "I never once heard them argue," he always said. What was her secret? Her recipe for the perfect marriage? This was what I'd come to discover, but I already knew her secret: She hadn't married a philandering, domineering prick like I had. And as I waited in the cold, ear-numbing silence, it occurred to me that Dee Dee might not know what to say to a woman who had.

It also occurred to me that she might not wish to speak to her granddaughter, that she was snubbing me. Before my wedding, my father had told me that she would not at all have approved of my marrying a Catholic. Dee Dee had been a staunch Methodist. She had lived around the corner from the Grace United Methodist Church and attended services every Sunday. During the week, she had been a devoted member of the Ladies Auxiliary, a group best known for the recipe books they put out every year. On my wedding day, Dee Dee might have rolled over in her casket, turning a bony shoulder to me forever, though I preferred to think that the dead rose above the petty prejudices they held in life.

Methodist, Catholic—it was all the same to me. Organized religion did nothing for me. Nature was my religion, *Pilgrim at Tinker Creek* my bible, and though I did not consider myself an atheist, I thought it was silly to personify the divine force of the universe. Of course, this left me with no "God" to talk to—just a dead woman in a cemetery. A very reticent one, apparently.

"Dee Dee, are you there?"

What did two women, two generations apart, have to say to one another, anyway? Sara Parry Davies was born in 1892, in the last gasp of the Victorian era, not far from Gallipolis. Her roles as a woman would have been clear to her, though growing up on a farm, she was probably less constrained than many women of her era. She went to the local college to study piano for a year—or was it longer? The record is fuzzy on this. She became a wife and mother and, in accordance with the expectations of the time, was skillful in performing her roles. She was very "capable," as my father liked to put it. I, on the other hand, was born in 1955, near the beginning of the era that would question almost everything my grandparents' generation believed in. Presumably, the women of my generation were freer to choose our destinies, to move into the realm of men if we so chose. It seemed that my world and Dee Dee's couldn't have been more different.

And yet, in ways I don't understand and probably never will, Victorian culture had always fascinated me. Even as a child, I loved old houses and dreamed of living in one myself some day. After I graduated from college, my philandering husband and I ended up renting a drafty old Victorian from my in-laws. We called it "May Woods's house" for the woman who had lived there for decades into her dotage and whose spirit permeated its thick walls still covered in variations of gray wallpaper. In the summers, I would stay up late into the night reading of the plights of Victorian heroines created by Charlotte Brönte and Thomas Hardy. I identified with them. I would collect antiques and refinish them myself—my therapy for a rotten marriage. I would find it satisfying to strip off the thick, murky layers of varnish to see the grain and light hiding in the wood underneath.

"Dee Dee, *please.*"

I uttered my petition one last time, like a prayer to a god who may or may not be there. I waited and waited. Nothing. Apparently, I had no talent for channeling the dead.

"OH, DEE DEE, maybe it's just as well you didn't answer me that day."

Now it was clear that divorcing Richard all those years ago had been the right thing to do. But it was doubtful Dee Dee would've steered me in that direction. More likely, she would've told me to hang in there. But staying in that marriage would have been deadening. And as much as I loved Gallipolis, living there all those years probably would have been, too. I shuddered imagining what my life might have been like if I had.

But even though Dee Dee hadn't responded to my pleas for help, I may have come to associate the cemetery with her, thinking of it as a place of grandmotherly nurturance and comfort.

No wonder I ended up being a taphophile.

I had gone to Mound Hill all those years ago to seek marital advice, but really, I was looking for something far more essential: Myself. Or rather, some stronger, clearer version of myself. My Inner Dee Dee. As well as a maternal legacy of strength.

In my treks through various cemeteries, was I looking for that still?

Knocking on Death's Door

On a mausoleum door made of bronze, green with age,
is the face of a woman wearing a crown of poppies. Her eyes
are closed as if she's dead or dormant and dreaming, and
surrounding her chin is a thick ℧ meant for knocking.
    It is Persephone, Goddess of the Underworld.

> *What would happen if I knocked?*
> *Is there a special password for entrance?*

Say *Pomegranate* and Hades is yours.

Death's Bride

They never wanted you to know
the hunger of Persephone,
how she starved for something
other than pomegranates.
~ Emily Palermo

SHADEVILLE. BY ALL appearances from Route 23, one of those little "don't blink or you'll miss it" bergs. Or maybe you just couldn't see it from the road. But you could see St. Joseph's and Mt. Calvary, which side by side look like one big cemetery. Shadeville, as if that's where you'll find "the shades," as Homer called them, vapors in the mist.

It was a cold, dreary day in December, halfway between the end of Autumn Quarter and Christmas, that deadly season when I think I can accomplish an impossible multitude of feats—household catch-up, Christmas cards and shopping, volumes of writing, darkroom printing, a to-do list a mile long that even the Bionic Woman wouldn't attempt. And this year, a job application to add to the list. I was supposed to slip into a promotion for a full-time position at a branch of Ohio University, but the rules had changed, and now a national search had to be done, forcing me to compete for a position I had already earned. Despite the reassurance I had received by my colleagues in English, I was nervous about it. It was my last chance. And since Ben had recently lost his job, it was doubly important that I get the position. Eventually, I did, thank God and the heavens.

That morning, I had woken up with the blues. I needed a fix. Shadeville. Just a few miles south of Columbus. The weather made it impractical to go any further away than that. But I needed to go somewhere. Shadeville. I was overcome with a longing to go there.

IT WAS A lousy day for shooting statues. Without sun, they looked horribly flat. But it wasn't a bad day for shooting grave portraits, I soon discovered. No sun, no glare. St. Joe's was full of such portraits. Many Italian-Americans are buried there. And I have noticed it's primarily Greeks and Italians who have a fondness for mounting the photographs of the deceased on their headstones. The images—usually black-and-white, often brown-toned—are fired on to a smooth oval of ceramic, porcelain or metal, and later embellished with a design cut into the surrounding stone. Ever since seeing Little Bastiani's grave portrait when I was a child, I had found these portraits fascinating and hauntingly beautiful. Aesthetically speaking, shooting them felt a bit like cheating, though aesthetics isn't the only motive. You have to shoot them straight on, no fancy angles. And there's something redundant about taking a photograph of a photograph. But I shot them anyway; I couldn't resist.

I moved from portrait to portrait. From infants to children to adults, until I came to the photograph that moved me like no other: the bridal portrait of a woman who had died when she was only twenty nine.

PASQUA MARINELLA SERGIO

MOGLIE DI

MICHELE SERGIO

NATA IL 6 GENNAIO 1895,

MORTA IL 17 GENNAIO 1924

"She's so beautiful," I whispered to God and the shades from the past. Tears filled my eyes at the unfairness of her passing. "So beautiful."

I guessed the wedding portrait had been taken when she was younger and was quite possibly the only formal photograph her husband had to put on her gravestone. I recognized the vintage style of the white shirtwaist dress and shoes from the 1920s, but never having seen a headdress like the one she wore in the photograph—a wide spray of fabric that covered the head from ear to ear and sat low on the brow—I wondered if it was peculiar to Italians. (Later I'd realize it was a popular twenties style.) She held a large floral arrangement in her left hand. Most noticeable, she was not smiling in the portrait. In fact, in the closed-lip set of her mouth, I saw grim resignation, and in her eyes, I saw fear.

Of course, I knew from seeing my paternal grandparents' wedding portrait that people of that generation didn't smile for photographs, especially not for formal sittings. And the expression a person happens to be wearing the minute the shutter releases isn't necessarily a reliable reflection of his or her mood that day or even the moment after the picture was taken. Nevertheless, I believed that Pasqua was unhappy on her wedding day. And I felt certain she became disillusioned and disappointed in the years that followed. Perhaps by the time she died at twenty nine, she felt dead already. For some, marriage becomes deadening.

Was I projecting? My own marriage was difficult and disappointing by then. That was another reason I had the blues that day, and most days. Eight years my junior, Ben was immature, contentious, and unambitious. Our almost daily clashes were stressful. Secretly, I wondered if I'd made a mistake and should leave, though I felt guilty having such thoughts. Nevertheless, looking at the wedding portrait of the unhappy young bride that day, I didn't understand why it touched me so deeply. I found my response puzzling.

In a way, my confusion made sense. Memorial portraits such as Pasqua's *are* confusing to look at. And therein lies their power. Usually taken on a momentous occasion or milestone of the deceased person's life, the photograph engages us in a present that is now long past. Later, mounted onto a gravestone, the photo once meant to celebrate a moment has now been reframed to memorialize that person's life. The dual purpose creates a contradiction that confuses the emotions in the person looking at the photo. Simultaneously feeling connected and separated, we experience cognitive/emotional dissonance. As Ron Horne puts it, "Memorial portraits place you on the boundary of time but you are not sure which side you are standing on."

"She's so beautiful," I whispered as I got into the car, now sobbing, my heart heavy with sorrow for her. Only vaguely did I sense that when I wept for Pasqua, I wept for myself and every woman who had ever married and felt disillusioned.

Ode to the Necromancers
(For Dogs & Memoirists)

Oh, these necromancers who groom the past so doggedly,
who with twitchy nose and itchy paw
sense every living vibration,
who seek their salvation in the corpses of memory
with canine intensity,
who eat death like a delicacy to be transformed
into blood and the fiber of life,
who chase the dream into the dark brush and
flit from tree to tree with ferocious
exuberance for the mere sake of it,
who run bounding for the mere joy of it,
with the innocent greed of children
for a taste of life and knowledge.
For these and other such skills,
Mandy is my role model.

Wait for Me

You ask of my companions.
Hills, sir, and the sundown,
and a dog as large as myself.
~Emily Dickinson

I think of Heaven as a garden where I shall find
again those dear ones who have made my world.
~ Minnie Aumônier

I HAVE SAID so much about the cemetery as a spiritual landscape, but what I most want to tell you is how much I loved walking through Woodlawn Cemetery with Mandy, my beautiful black flatty. How I loved watching her gallop free through the grounds, her feathers flying back in the breeze her running made while chasing a squirrel up a tree or a groundhog to its hole in the earth. Then, the stomp of her forelegs on the ground and a smile of satisfaction, as if to say, *There! I've done my job.* She'd romp here and there, from path to hill and over yonder, a diagonal zigzag following only her interests, occasionally stopping for minutes at a time to study a scent. She was a connoisseur of all things stinky—oh, how she savored garbage!—a scholar of the schnoz.

Me, I was more likely to have my nose in a book. I tend to be overly mental, to live in my head, as Mandy could have told you, having so often waited for me while I read or wrote. "Hang in there," I'd tell her. "Just a few more minutes," minutes turning to hours. I needed to move around, get physical. Without her need or nudging, it's unlikely I would've started walking anywhere, much less through cemeteries.

DURING WALKS ALSO, I would frequently ask Mandy to wait. Unlike getting a dog to come on command, getting a dog to wait is something I've always been able to pull off. "Wait for me," I'd tell her when she was romping ahead of me off leash, and then she'd wait until I caught up. But two years after our move to Columbus, it become less necessary to ask her to wait.

I first noticed Mandy slowing down during a return visit to Woodlawn, made to renew my inspiration. It had taken way longer to make our rounds than it had in the past. On our daily constitutionals in the park near home, too, she seemed to plod along. She was by now thirteen—a good long lifespan for a large dog and especially flatties who, predisposed to liver cancer, don't often make it past eight. I figured being a mixed breed was probably to her advantage. I assumed her slowing down was caused by a touch of arthritis.

During one walk in the park that summer, I happened to glance up at a branch overhead to see an owl staring down at us. It was chunky, with fluffy buff feathers and large black circles ringing its dark hungry eyes. Most likely a young barred owl. This was the first owl I'd seen in the woods. It was only five in the afternoon, and it surprised me that I should see the nocturnal bird so early in the day.

"Mandy, look!" I said, hoping to share my excitement.

But she was oblivious. I remembered that, on another day, a deer had leapt across the path just a few yards in front of her, and she hadn't noticed that either. I amended my diagnosis: Cataracts, perhaps, along with the arthritis.

Having seen my first owl, I was now thoroughly smitten and began looking for them daily, scanning the branches overhead, though they're more likely to be spotted first in flight, with their slow, steady glide through the air.

Then one evening, I began to wish I'd never see the owl in the woods that day. I was watching a movie featuring Native Americans, who see owls as omens of death. And I began to wonder if the owl I saw foretold the death of someone close to me. But who? Who might it be? One of our elderly parents? Another relative? A friend? It didn't occur to me that it might be Mandy.

By mid-September, Mandy's slowing gait led us to the vet, who ordered sonograms and X-rays. Cancer had eaten away at her insides to such an extent that surgery was not even an option. We were stunned. In the weeks that followed, her decline was so rapid it made our heads spin. For so many years, she had been a beloved member of the family, and it was hard to imagine our lives without her. By November, Mandy was gaunt, her face hollowed out, and her muzzle whitening beyond its natural markings. And the most shocking change of all: the gluttonous flatty—who had once carried a loaf of French bread she'd found *dans la bouche* for twelve blocks—had lost her appetite.

We debated whether or not we should have her put down. The vet, Dr. April (so called to distinguish her from Dr. Joe, her husband and business partner) gently supported the idea as the most humane option. But when? My previous dog, Fin, had given me "the look," a sad expression that said *I'm in terrible pain; please do something. I'm ready to go.* By that time, she had also lost control of her functions and could only eat nutritional gel from a tube presented on fingertip, signs that made the decision so much easier. I kept waiting for the go-ahead from Mandy, too, but despite her obvious discomfort, "the look" never came. We were simply going to have to make the call. Finally, we scheduled a Saturday morning appointment for Dr. April to put her to sleep.

The strange thing about a scheduled death is that it grants you a special prescience you normally wouldn't have. In the case of euthanizing a dog, you know which meal or walk or wade in the creek will be the last, even while they do not, and the poignancy of this discrepancy is almost unbearable.

Even though her appetite had been very poor, that last night she consumed the better part of a half-pound steak and dish of vanilla ice cream with relish. *That's my girl!* The next morning—a gorgeous autumn day—I watched as she lay under the deep red leaves of the Japanese maple on the edge of the patio, innocently enjoying the day as best she could. A line of poetry came to mind, "someone today is

seeing the world for the last time as innocently as he had seen it first."[17]
It satisfied my need for words that would describe the situation and
her innocence, which is what I value most in the canine species. We
took her for one last walk in the neighborhood park, where she and I
had walked so many times. She waded in the creek for a while. And
then it was time.

Ben was beside himself as Dr. April began the injection. We each
held a paw and wept. Feeling both guilt and grief, Ben said, "I'm sorry,
Mandy." More certain that it was the right thing to do, I simply tried
to offer comfort, "Ah, poor Mandy. It'll be all right." Dr. April and the
vet techs assisting her gave us a few moments to say goodbye in private.
Then they returned to wrap her in the soft baby blue blanket we had
brought and put her in the trunk for us. Technically it was illegal to bury
your dog in your backyard, as we planned to do, but no one questioned
what we intended to do with her body. The following week, they would
send a sympathy note.

WITH EVERY PLUNGE of his shovel, Ben hit stone. He was
digging just beyond the fence line overlooking the creek, so of course
the ground was rocky. The truth of this might have been evident in the
various large specimens that adorned the front yard and garden. But
these brown oblong stones looked more like potatoes, and Ben pulled
one after another from the hole that would become Mandy's grave.
Later we would use them to create barriers between Mandy's remains
and scavenging varmints inclined to dig them up, place the rest around
the edge for a decorative border.

"This is going to take hours," he warned. "A pickaxe would be better.
Think I'll run to Home Depot and buy one."

I felt bad that he was doing all the work, but my back couldn't handle
the strain. All I could do was offer moral support and gather memories
while I waited.

I hadn't planned on adopting a large dog, but when I went to the
pound in Bloomington, she had been the only one among them not
yapping her fool head off. Even at six months, she was much calmer
than the high strung sheepdog mix I had briefly considered. When I
stood in front of her cage, looking into her eyes, a thought came to

mind: *This dog's name is "Mutsy" or "Mugsy"... something like that.* Sure enough, a staff member told me her name had been "Mutley." Pretty darn close. If I thought Mandy and I had a telepathic connection, that clinched it.

Thinking "Mutley" undignified, I decided to retain the "M" and change the rest of the name. As I put her into the backseat of the car, I tried out "Mo" but quickly discovered it sounded too much like "No!" and would be confusing. Then I landed on "Mandy." That seemed a good fit. My friend Ann said it made her think of the Barry Manilow song, which she considered a drawback. *Oh Mandy, you gave and you gave without taking, but I sent you away . . .* Okay, corny, but I'd found out that her family had given her up, so maybe that sort of fit, too. Their loss.

I remembered how, oddly, Mandy remained mute for several weeks after I brought her home. "What's wrong, Mandy," I'd joke, "cat got your tongue?" Hehe. Then finally, she emitted a deep full-throated bark that would scare the bejesus out of anyone who might dare to trespass our threshold. Which was a good thing, since beyond that, it was unlikely she'd be much of a threat. Her forte was making friends.

I thought of all the friends Mandy had made over the years. As a big black dog, she had to overcome the fear some people felt when first seeing her. Her secret was in the tail. She'd wag it until her entire rear end moved from side to side—a literal enactment of the tail wagging the dog. That last year in Bloomington, I'd leave her outside the post office tied to the fence railing in front, only to return to see her with a newly made friend petting her, tail and rear swishing blissfully from side to side. Our neighbor, Bob, a retired fellow with a West Virginian accent, made over her every time he entered his side door, which was right next to the fence in our yard. I could still hear his morning greeting: "Hi there, Mandy. How's my sweetheart doin' today?" He and his wife ate out frequently, and he'd offer the leftovers to her—fried chicken, spaghetti, and the like—delectables that, frankly, I would've kept for myself. During the Year in Hell, the two little girls from next door would actually knock on the door asking, "Can Mandy come out and play?" So sweet it made my eyes water.

I remembered how she'd pause by the garbage can in the house in Beantown to cop a whiff of some stinky, rotting something (there being neither shower nor garbage disposal in the house on Hazel), and have a field day getting into the garbage can when we weren't home and had neglected to set it out of reach behind the basement door.

She was Demanding Mandy when she clanged her metal bowl to let me know she needed water. Subtle Mandy when she simply sat beside it, patiently waiting. Stealth Mandy, as Ben called her when he shot video of her in Woodlawn while she hid behind a tree in wait for a groundhog.

I was laughing aloud, when Ben looked over at me and stopped shoveling.

"What?" he asked.

"Oh, I was just remembering how Mandy reacted to the rumble strips that time when we went down to visit Mom and Dad."

"Oh my God, that was so funny!"

We both pictured the look of surprise on her face when the car ran over the rumble strips in the sharp curve of the road, vibrating to the noise the strips made: *zzzzrt! zzzzrt! zzzzrt!*

Mandy had been so important to our marriage. We had even taken her along on our honeymoon to Kelleys Island. In some ways, she had been the glue that held us together—what Doris Lessing called the mystical third that every couple needs to balance the dyad, usually a child but sometimes a project or surrogate—or pet. I wondered how losing her would impact our relationship. I wondered how long I'd be able to stand living without a dog.

HOLY SCAVENGER. GENTLE goof and jester. Innocence incarnate . . . Angel and guide.

Oh Mandy, I thought, you have been with me through it all: the dissertation years, the Year in Hell at the liberal arts college, the move to Beantown, the tenure denial and the move to Columbus. Your constant companionship was such a comfort. And now that you are gone, that cycle of my life is also coming to an end. No longer will I be saying to you, as I did every night, "Goodnight, Mandy. I'll see you in the morning."

Around eleven that night, Ben finished digging the hole, and we went to get Mandy's body, wrapped in her blanket shroud, from the garage. We placed her gently into the grave—along with her collar, a couple of daisies that happened to bloom the day before, a poem Ben had written for her, and a note I had written—then together added the layers of soil and stone. After we were done, Ben wanted to sprinkle some wildflower seeds over the top, in hopes they would bloom in the spring. (They didn't.)

Toward the end of the process, now close to midnight, we heard an owl hooting in a nearby tree. *Hoo, hoo, hoo. H-hoo, H-hoooo* . . . Over and over. *This is who I warned you about . . .* And I thought of the words I had written in my note to my beloved canine companion. *Thank you for being such a good dog, Mandy. I love you. Wait for me.* And somehow, I knew she would.

Requiem for a Poet

Dear Nan,

Went to your memorial service today. There was quite a turn-out. The campus auditorium was nearly filled. You would've been pleased. The weather cooperated. On the long drive there, up to the flatland neither of us was fond of, fog everywhere, drizzle. Appropriately gloomy. We read the poems in which you are dancing. I read your harlequin poem, the one you wrote on the back of the faculty meeting agenda. You can just imagine Hyacinth's reaction to that. I love thinking of you as "the mad harlequin, dancing on the street corner," free from your wheelchair at last. Free from that cage of twisted bones, the site of so much pain. We even played a little Marley at the end. Later, at the restaurant, we toasted you with shots of black Jack, just as you would have wanted. *To Nan!* Clink, clank. *To Nan! To Nan!*

On the drive back home, your words ran through my head. *I do not want to spend my life Xeroxing page upon page of other people's poems to give uninterested students . . . Let me sing instead like the mad harlequin . . . Let my language clang in time to the tambourine hanging at my knee, let it ring in tunes small and bright.* I saw you dressed in diamonds of color, *bells stitched to* your *shirttails.* I saw you *whirling and chanting in rhythm,* hopping toe to toe in the spotlight cast on the highway just ahead. *Let me sing . . . like the mad harlequin . . . in tunes small and bright. Let me sing . . . Dancing.*

As I approached Columbus, the sky began to clear, and I inserted my North Mississippi Allstars CD. Cute boys playing Southern blues. Sensual, rousing, funny. I thought you would like it, thought it might remind you of home. This was as close to Tennessee as I could get. "Po Black Maddie, ain't got change of clothes, Fool got drunk, and throw'd the trunk outdoors." "I don't want skinny woman, Meat don't shake." "Need no heater or fireplace by my bed, The woman I got, keeps me cher-ry red." You could've danced to it.

The Healing Garden

It brings me total joy—total, total joy. When I leave here,
I am always more positive in what I go back to in life.
~ Barbara Collier, on visiting Cypress Lawn Cemetery[18]

I WAS CHATTING with Ryan, the quiet young man who operated
the camera for an interview filmed by a colleague of mine about my
work on cemeteries. We were filming in Grandview Cemetery, near the
campus where I taught in Chillicothe.

"I think more women than men are drawn to cemeteries," I said to
him. "We seem to have a special connection."

"Yeah, it's a girl thing," he replied. Ryan was an alternative type, and
since many taphies are too, I figured his opinion was an informed one.

The conversation reminded me of a paper I'd received a couple of
years before written by another alternative student named Jessica. It was
about her struggle with anorexia and the role Grandview played in her
recovery.

"Include photographs of yourself to document it," I remembered
suggesting. But once she turned in the paper, I dreaded looking at them.
I didn't want to see her wasted away. I'd been right to suggest it, though.
The photos were so vivid I still remembered them.

In the first set, she was a typical high school girl—talking on the
phone, dancing at the prom with her boyfriend, sucking on a cigarette,

laughing with friends—with weight progressively dropping: 135 . . . 130 . . . 125 . . . 120. A straighter, thinner version of the punked out kid in black who sat in the front of my classroom twice a week, but essentially the same young woman with the dark, shiny eyes, animated and funny.

On the next page, photos of an emaciated girl I barely recognized: 87 pounds. In one, she wore red plaid slacks and a black turtleneck sweater that hung loose on her bony frame. Both the outfit and her emaciation were shocking to see. At the top of the page, she had written, *The Skeleton*, and that was exactly what she looked like. A skeleton wearing red plaid slacks and a black turtleneck. A spector of the girl I was so fond of. Only the eyes were the same.

And then, the photos I didn't expect: photographs of Jessica and a companion in a cemetery at night, taking turns to pose here and there. He wore a black t-shirt that said "Necrophilia." She wore a black shirt and blue jeans, her hair cut short, a couple of earrings in each lobe—a demi-goth in the making. At first I didn't get it. What were they doing there? Why had she included these pictures? Then I saw the title: *The Healing Garden*. Visiting the cemetery had nourished her and healed her. In the final photograph, she is squatting in front of a gravestone, as if ready to sprint into life, smiling, eyes glistening. Resurrection.

I was not a recovering anorexic, but I was a recovering academic. I knew something about starving. What woman didn't? And I knew about the healing power of Victorian cemeteries.

"We are Sisters of the Grave," I told her when returning the paper, smiling.

She nodded, smiling back.

I WAS BEGINNING to believe there were quite a few of us in what seemed like a secret sorority. Female taphophilia dated back to as early as 1835, when Mary Tyler Peabody gushed her praises of Mount Auburn in that letter to her girlfriend: "How can I describe the feeling with which I looked again upon our gorgeous woods and heard the song of the wind in the pine groves? . . . I always feel as if I want to stay when I get there." And it continued into the twentieth century and into the present. I didn't think it was an accident that there were twice as many women as men enrolled as members of the Association of Gravestone Studies.

Of course the two people who had initiated me into taphophilia— Jane and Macky—were women, so no wonder that I had always thought of it as a girl thing. But I continued to meet women who confirmed the theory first hand. Not only Jessica, but another woman, Skip Hathaway, whom I met at a poetry reading on campus. I had read a lyrical riff or two about the magic of printing cemetery photos, and so after the reading, she approached me to tell me about the Tombstone Club.

"Well, you might be interested in this," she began. "Some ladies here started it. After a woman's husband dies, they pick out the tombstone together and then go up to the cemetery to celebrate. They take a picnic lunch, spread out a blanket, and make a party out of it." I wondered if they had been inspired by the Broadway play *The Cemetery Club*, which was later made into a film.

"In Grandview?" I asked.

"That's right. Oh, it's great," she replied.

"Wow. That *is* interesting." Yep, pretty interesting, all right.

Skip didn't explain it, but I gathered that the party wasn't to celebrate the passing of the spouse, but rather to soften the blow. I thought of it as a rite of passage more intimate than the formality of the official funeral service, where decorum tends to keep tears and other public expressions of grief in check.

There were also books—lots of wonderful cemetery-inspired books!—that confirmed my theory. I had already gobbled up Tracy Chevalier's novel, *Falling Angels*, which captures female taphophilia perfectly in Maude and Lavinia, her turn-of-the-century characters who run wild through England's Highgate. As Maude says, "It was such a treat to be in the cemetery without anyone to look after us. Whenever I go with Mummy and Daddy or Grandmother, I feel I have to be very quiet and solemn, when really what I want to do is just what Lavinia and I did—rush about and explore." *Exactly.* Chevalier herself fell in love with Highgate Cemetery, saying, "I loved the quiet and beauty of the place. It definitely got under my skin." She offered her services there as tour guide and gardener (read: weeder), and continued even after finishing the novel.

Later I'd read Audrey Niffenegger's Highgate-inspired novel, *Fearful Symmetry*, about twin girls who end up living next to it. Niffenegger, an alternative, nerdy sort of girl herself, had always been preoccupied with old cemeteries. Recalling a special moment, she said, "I have an incredible memory of visiting Highgate Cemetery in June. It was a bright day and it was green, it was lush, but it was broken. I fell in love with it" and "was smitten with the notion of writing about this place."[19] I knew the feeling. Except for the brokenness, she might have been describing Woodlawn. Like Chevalier, she became a tour guide at Highgate, which she finds "thrilling." She is such a devoted taphophile, she included a request for donations for the upkeep and preservation of Highgate on the novel's last page, noting, "Sumptuous cemeteries are expensive to maintain, alas." In 2009, Highgate's upkeep ran £1000 a day.

I had also devoured Sarah Stewart Taylor's delightful mystery series that features Sweeney St. George, amateur sleuth and Harvard professor, specializing in cemetery art and mourning jewelry, which helps her to solve the cases. And there's Amada Stewart's Graveyard Queen series, which features a cemetery restorer. Not to mention Charlaine Harris's graphic novel trilogy, *Cemetery Girl*. And Sandra Russell Clark's lush *Elysium* takes my breath away. Her sepia-tinted infrared art photos of New Orleans cemeteries capture the feminine sensibility I longed to capture in my own photographs.

I found a number of websites set up by female taphies. The most impressive is Beth Santore's graveaddiction.com, which painstakingly catalogues hundreds of cemeteries she's visited over the years, primarily in Ohio, complete with coordinates and dropdown menus featuring photos of interesting monuments in each one. "Putting the 'Rave' Back in Grave," the Gravestone Girls sell jewelry, magnets and decorative items ("Art for the Here-Life," they call it) made from castings of stones in New England. Sabrina's Graveyard also offers goods (mugs, patches, pins, postcards and such) made from rubbings of New England gravestones. Later, I'd attend one of her gravestone rubbing workshops at an AGS conference, a.k.a. "Cemetery Camp," reminding me of cemetery expeditions we used to take in Girl Scout camp. The Cemetery Club is yet another website, set up by Minda Powers-Douglas as a way for taphies to connect.

Even though I wasn't predisposed to decorating my home in Cemetery Goth motif, the Gothic Martha Stewart site, offering "DIY décor for the morbidly inclined" was an especially cool find. "Ever want to live in a graveyard?" webmistress Trystan Bass asks. "If crumbling stonework and tattered shrouds appeal to you, there are many things you can do to make your home resemble the inside of a crypt." And as might be expected of the Gothic Martha Stewart, she offers well-organized advice and how-to instructions on just how to do it.

While I didn't decorate my home à la Goth, my study could be described as Victorian Gothique. Once we moved to the house by the park, I painted the study pink, filled it with cemetery-related knickknacks and framed cemetery prints for inspiration, and nicknamed it my Womb-Tomb. In *Magick, Myth, Fantasy & Romance*, an unsolicited catalog I recently received in the mail—obviously geared toward women—I thought I might have found another kitschy gem for my collection—a small resin replica of a weeping seraph sculpture. The description was tongue-in-cheek but surprisingly well-informed: "Inspired by memorials from the heyday of America's park cemetery movement, this weeping seraph expresses the grief (at times, seemingly unendurable) that compassionate friendship helps console." Yep, looked like it might be a good addition.

In her book, *The Cemetery Walk*, Minda Powers-Douglas tries to rally taphies: "Taphophiles Unite! We are the few, the proud, the obsessed. We love cemeteries, and we aren't ashamed to admit it. Well, maybe some of us are still worried that people might look at us funny. But we are what we are. We come in all personalities, shapes, and sizes. Just know, my fellow taphs, you are not alone." Truth be told, we are a rather secretive bunch. We are so secret, few of us know our other sisters, so it is comforting to know there are others out there. And I suspect its ambience of seclusion is another reason the cemetery appeals to women. As Niffennegger says, "You can walk around and be quite alone and hidden. I think novelists like secret places because we are so secretive ourselves." The enclosed "bower," to use a favorite nineteenth-century term, is a feminine space that is attractive to women, writers or not. We like the peace and quiet, along with dark humor and playful subversion. Being a taphie is fun.

Why else did Victorian cemeteries appeal to women?

Tracy Chevalier said she "fell in love with the decay, the gothic excess, the neglect" of Highgate.[20] Her affection for decay suggests a Wabi Sabi aesthetic which, like "shabby genteel," is often feminine in style, perhaps because tied to the Victorian era, which after all was ruled by a queen who was in mourning for forty years. In *Falling Angels,* Kitty Coleman, mother of the little taphophile, Maude, blames Queen Victoria for "elevating mourning to such ridiculous heights that girls with romantic notions grow drunk from it." The novel begins on the day after Queen Victoria died in 1901. Like me, Niffenegger appreciates the Victorian cemetery as an "urban nature preserve, full of rare butterflies and bold foxes," even noting the wonderful detail that, in Highgate, "there are buzzing new beehives on top of the terrace catacombs." She also observes that the cemetery is "a place where the sacred and historic intersect," while at the same time having a "mythic pull."

Are we women taphies tapping into the collective unconscious and its chthonic archetypes that connect women to the underworld? I thought of Psyche's tasks, which included crossing the Styx and visiting Persephone, Queen of the Underworld, for some of her special beauty ointment. I felt uncomfortable with the stereotype that linked women to earth and death in that way, but I couldn't deny that the archetype resonated with female taphophilia. The mythic dimension also connected to Goddess worship. Patricia Reis says, "In Goddess language, death is the prelude to rebirth."[21] This would be driven home to me in the future, when I travelled to Crete for a Goddess Pilgrimage led by Carol P. Christ, who taught us to think of the ancient goddess as Regeneratrix.[23]

And that was what was so powerful about Jessica's story. Like a Lady Lazarus, she had risen from the grave of anorexia, restored to life. And me, well, I was working toward my own resurrection. My own healing. In the cemetery.

Yeah, it was a girl thing for sure.

Why I ♥ Cemeteries

LET ME COUNT the reasons . . .

I love the Victorian cemetery for the natural beauty of the landscape, with its thick, green blanket of vegetation and the path looping through it like a soft, supple ribbon.

I love the fact that it is a multipurpose landscape meant to be enjoyed by the living, much like a park in which people walk their dogs, jog, ride bicycles, even fish. That it's both arboretum and bird sanctuary—a place for the wingéd creatures, be they feathered or human or angelic.

Yet I also love that it isn't merely a park, that it's also a burial ground, because that is what sanctifies the land and gives the place its depth, its layered significance. That is what makes the cemetery a sacred space.

I love that it's a place meant to comfort mourners who have lost loved ones or parts of themselves, that it soothes the brokenhearted and distraught. That the space is feminine and maternal. That the cemetery wraps her great, green arms around you and whispers there, there.

I love the artwork of the cemetery—the sculpture and architecture, the emblems carved in stone—that it's an outdoor art museum and that I might find any number of surprises when exploring a cemetery that's new to me.

I love that the landscape architects who designed the Victorian Garden Cemetery did not evade the fact of death but shifted the paradigm from Grim Reaper to Gentle Farmer who reaps what S/He has sown and then gathers us home. That this garden they created manifests the miraculous cycle of life and death and regeneration, and exults it. That they deliberately created a space to inspire reverence and reflection. That it's a garden for the soul.

I love the cemetery for being the place where heaven and earth meet, the site where horizontal and vertical converge in sacred crossing. That it's the home of Both/And, not Either/Or.

I love that the cemetery is inherently symbolic and archetypal, of the larger scheme of things as well as my own life. That following its path has enabled me to exhume and reclaim parts of myself I have buried. That it has given me license to embrace the spiritual dimension of life and continue the quest that is my birthright.

I love how the cemetery embodies the Sacred, makes it tangible and real.

I love that the cemetery is my Muse.

Descent

> The underworld aspect of each complex is . . .
> where the soul can be refound.
>   ~ James Hillman, *The Dream and the Underworld*

I STOOD AT the back door gazing into the darkness, mulling over the frustration I'd had that day. Once again, I had spent hours trying to figure out why I was so obsessed with cemeteries, Woodlawn in particular.

That afternoon, Ben had offered his take on it.

"I think Woodlawn represents all that you lost in Beantown," he said. "Beantown was the last place where you had stability. You had a good job that you loved. Colleagues and friends. You made a decent salary. You had status. And Woodlawn was the place you were most attached to there."

"Yeah, I suppose so," I'd replied.

I knew there was more to it. Something more personal and private than a job. More fundamental. For some time, I had been excavating my life, my pen like a spade plumbing the depths. But I kept feeling that I was missing something.

What is it? What is it? What have I forgotten to unbury?

I was so frustrated, I started crying, then hyperventilating. The more I gulped for air, the more agitated I became.

I was in the middle of a full-fledged panic attack.

Hearing strange noises coming from the family room, Ben rushed in from the kitchen.

"What's wrong?"

"I—can't—breathe," I stammered in between gasps.

He stood in the doorway, dumbfounded, clueless about what to do.

"I—can't—talk—very—well," I said. I motioned for him to come sit on the couch, irked that, in the midst of a panic attack, I had to orchestrate my own care. "Hold—my hand."

We sat this way until the worst subsided and I could explain what triggered the attack.

"It seems to me, you're putting a lot of pressure on yourself," he said. "You need to rest. I thought that's why you took the summer off from teaching."

"You're probably right . . ." I had wanted a break from teaching, but I had also hoped to make miraculous progress on the book.

"You should take a whole week off before teaching starts again. Just do nothing."

"Uh-huh." A whole week? It sounded good, but . . .

"Seriously."

I HAD WANTED to make faster progress on writing the book, but the truth was, there was more than a book at stake. I was undergoing a spiritual journey where timelines don't apply. So, as Ben suggested, I allowed myself to put the book aside for a while, but I continued to read and study.

What are the steps of a spiritual journey? In Joseph Campbell's classic model, the hero hears a call, leaves home to encounter tests and trials, then reaps a reward and returns home to share the boon. But this didn't quite fit what I had been going through. According to Maureen Murdock, the heroine's journey involves not only ordeal but also a descent to the realm of the underworld (the subconscious) to reclaim the feminine, sacrificed in order to succeed in the masculine milieu, and to repair the mother-daughter split. During her descent, a woman may dream of wombs and tombs, of goddesses and their emblems. In the underworld, one "is naked and walks on the bones of the dead."[22] Bingo! I had visited tombs in person, photographed goddesses, literally walked on the bones of the dead (though not naked). Maybe I'd already descended then? I wasn't sure.

In her discussion of the descent, Murdock foregrounds the myth of Demeter and Persephone, which perfectly illustrates the reunion of mother and daughter and the healing of the wounded feminine. The goddess Demeter went to great lengths to find her daughter, Persephone, who had been abducted by Hades to the underworld. Maybe as the writer, I (like Demeter) was rescuing the younger me I was writing about (Persephone) from the dark, dank hell of academia. Yeah, that kind of made sense. And the cemetery might represent my subconscious, where the rejected parts of myself are buried. Maybe.

I soaked up these ideas like a flower parched for rain. But at the end of the day, thinking isn't the same as having an experience. The journey can't be made through intellect. So finally, after intense study, I was ready to put it all away. I'd focus on photography instead. Go over to the darkroom to do some printing. Do a couple of photoshoots. Go to the garden cemetery in Mansfield. Revisit Woodlawn. Maybe I'd find some answers there. Even a revelation. One could always hope.

LEE, A COLLEAGUE at the darkroom, kept insisting I shoot at the National Shrine of Our Lady of Consolation in Carey.

"There's a very impressive bronze statue of Mary there," she said. "I really think you'd like it."

Why not? A shrine isn't a cemetery but not altogether unlike one either. And Carey wasn't far from Beantown. I could shoot there, hit Maple Grove in Findlay, then end up at Woodlawn.

Once inside the basilica, I felt uncomfortable taking photographs. Wasn't it against the rules? But I noticed several other people doing so. One couple even asked me to take their picture as they posed in front of the basilica's altar.

Our Mother of Sorrows, the life-sized bronze of the grief-stricken Mary Lee was so eager for me to shoot, was a work of art, just as she had said. Wearing mannish shoes and a heavy robe with a hood that partially covered her face, she sat solid like a mountain of strength. She was a powerful presence, her grief palpable. I shot a roll, imagining how great the prints would look toned a rich brown. But she didn't move me as much as I expected.

In search of a bathroom, I made my way to the basement, where I felt drawn to a large, vacant room. At the front was a makeshift altar set up on a simple wooden table, featuring a framed print of the icon of Mary, Our Mother of Perpetual Help, with rows of folding chairs facing it and votive candles in the back. The energy was strong there, and I felt that this was a more authentic place of worship than the basilica upstairs.

In the painting, Mary's head is adorned with an immense crown, tiny angels hovering on either side. Her deep blue robe is studded with stars symbolizing her divinity. She holds her baby son in the crook of one arm, the hand of the other clasping his tiny hands to steady his perch. The child looks like a miniature adult and, forgetting who he was for a moment, I mistook him for a girl, a daughter instead of a son. With a subtle smile, Mary's face expresses the joy only a mother can know.

Ah, but the eyes . . . the eyes are what got to me. Somehow the turn of Mary's head and eyes gives the impression that she is looking right at you, that she extends her maternal solicitude and compassion toward you and anyone else who looks upon her. You can almost hear her saying, *I love you and feel for you. I will help you in any way I can. All you need do is ask. And you can ask for anything, anything at all.*

Mary's knowing expression struck me to the very core. I was so moved, I wept. It was such a relief to feel comforted, nurtured, even held by Mary, which is how it felt to be held in her gaze.

I scribbled a petition on a scrap of paper from a stack on the table (*Dear Mary, please give me the clarity I need to understand this journey*), then placed it in the basket on the table in front of the painting. I was so shaky, I sat down in one of the folding chairs to compose myself. Then, before leaving, I lit votive candles for my parents, Ben, and myself.

It was late afternoon by the time I drove to Maple Grove in Findlay. And it was there that I got further hung up. I found a bas relief of a goddess-like woman lowering a drape of cloth—She Who Rends the Veil, I called her—and decided to wait for the sun to illuminate her face and bring out her features for a sharper image. But really, I needed to move along to Woodlawn, and I could have kicked myself for not leaving sooner.

THE BEST IS YET TO BE
THE LAST OF LIFE FOR WHICH
THE FIRST WAS MADE

DRIVING THROUGH BEANTOWN, I was reminded of just how bleak it was. In fact, it looked even worse than I remembered. The whole town seemed covered with a thin coat of dust. *Note to self: Whenever you feel perversely nostalgic or weepy over Beantown, just go back and drive through as a reminder of what it's really like.*

In stark contrast, Woodlawn would be an oasis of green in the Beantonian desert, just as it had been that first August Mandy and I walked there over a decade ago. It had now been a couple of years since my last visit there with Mandy. Would I feel the same about it? Would it live up to the mythic proportions it had reached in my imagination?

It was near dusk, which meant I had only twenty minutes before invisible hands slowly drew the gates to an automatic close for the night, leaving very little time to do or see much of anything.

As I drove through the gate, I saw a bronze plaque—new since the last visit—with raised letters reading NO DOGS ALLOWED.

No dogs allowed?

I couldn't believe it. I had walked in Woodlawn Cemetery with Mandy for seven years. I couldn't imagine not being able to walk there with her, or any other dog for that matter. But if I had been granted tenure and stayed in Beantown, that's the position I would have been in, reduced to sneaking her in with me on weekends when the office was closed.

I parked the car toward the end of the entrance road where the path branches off, near the Lady with Open Arms. I was determined to get another good look at her. Were her eyes open or closed? Lately, I had been studying the photograph I had of her—one of the first I took—trying to verify which, but it was impossible to tell, even with a loop. *Open or closed?* For some reason, I needed to know.

I got out of the car, camera in tow, knowing full well the light was too dim to record a decent image, much less one sharp enough to reveal the status of her eyelids. She stands on a pedestal next to a tree and faces north to boot, moss tingeing her cheeks and robe; the light is never good from this angle. *Are her eyes open or closed?* I couldn't tell with naked eye or zoom, and there was no time to set up a tripod. But I shot her anyway, the light meter advising me not to.

What am I searching for? What is it I've forgotten to unbury?

As usual, I wanted to walk all the paths at once, renew acquaintance with my favorite monuments. But there was no time for that either. There was barely time for a quick drive through.

I looked over at the little stone houses on Mausoleum Row, which contained the Three Graces along with other beautiful stained glass windows, like secret gems hidden in fancy jewelry boxes. I noted the gnarly Catalpa nearby and remembered the pleasure of teaching American lit at the Twig in the fall (*Nevermore! Nevermore!*).

I drove back to the front and past the Dearly Departed monument, with the chiton-robed woman reading the tablet (EACH DEPARTED FRIEND IS A MAGNET THAT ATTRACTS US TO THE NEXT WORLD), which had reminded me of Ray when I first moved to Beantown and later Ted, once he was denied tenure and moved away,

Drove between Thompson and McCauley mausos (*Yea, though I walk through the valley of the shadow of death*), toward Gros Maire squatting on its island at the crossroads,

Hung a left to visit Brice and its solace (LET NOT YOUR HEART BE TROUBLED, NEITHER LET IT BE AFRAID), throwing a glance at the snarling lion atop the holding vault across the path, reminiscent of Jim Reaper,

Hastened toward the three Grandfather Pines, past the DAVIES monument (*there but for the grace of God go I*) and the Sad Little Lady on the verge of tears, holding her wreath, up the hill toward the community mauso overlooking the pond,

Headed toward the back corner to Mary Baker, whose affliction I had shared—saluting on the way the monolith of John Calvin, namesake of the building at the Twig that houses the English department and my old office—and to Lamenta looking down her nose at me and Mary, or so I imagined,

Noted the field left fallow for the future, save the small nursery of trees grown for replanting,

Onward toward the stony-faced sphinxes guarding the Michael family, the Taylor pyramid with its family crest, so oddly incongruous, the meadow below where Mandy liked to run and chase groundhogs,

Past the planter grave with finger pointing upward and over the bridge, seeing the stately BLACK monument to my right, topped with the woman leaning on her anchor with the dignity I coveted, a pink ribbon tied to the pillar in remembrance of the dead in summer.

Finally, I arrived back to the spot near the Lady with Open Arms to simply sit in the remaining minutes and register my emotions, still running close to the surface from my experience with Mary earlier in the day.

I felt choked up. I knew it was strange, but I couldn't help it. I missed Woodlawn. And I missed Mandy and walking there with her. So much it broke my heart.

Harvest

THE FIRST TIME I saw it, I was with Macky all those autumns ago on our photoshoot in Piqua. The monument was up on the hill in the back of the cemetery, not visible from the lower sections—an enormous sheaf of wheat carved in stone, bearing the inscription, *Gathered Home*.

The idea that, when we die, we are "gathered home" was comforting to me, as it is to many people. It suggests that our lives are not ruthlessly hacked by a grim fellow with a scythe, but gently gathered and gleaned by the Farmer who planted our soul, returning us to heaven, from whence we came.

Today, the giant sheaf of wheat reminds me of Demeter, Divine Mother and Goddess of Grain, who permitted the seasons to resume once she freed her daughter from the underworld and gathered her home, allowing once again a bountiful harvest. For my story, too, ends with harvest and homecoming and a kind of heaven.

Gathered Home

The descent into the depths always seems to precede the ascent.
~ Carl Jung

IF, ON THE deepest level, home is the place where you feel fully accepted for who you are, then homecoming still eluded me. I had a wonderful house in Columbus where I felt comfortable. I had finally found a job where I felt I could be myself in the classroom and had a solid prospect for a secure future, though admittedly, waiting for this to pan out was nerve wracking. But on that deeper psychic level of feeling accepted, I still found myself standing at the door, wiping my muddy feet on the welcome mat, waiting to be invited in. What would it take for me to be able to cross the threshold and be welcomed with open arms and a hug?

For so long, I thought achievement was the ticket. If I earned my Ph.D., if I got tenure, if I published a book . . . if, if, if . . . then I would gain not only my parents' acceptance but also their respect. Even after my panic attack, I found myself thinking that way. I was still haunted by Dad saying several years before that I hadn't proven myself to him yet. But if being welcomed into the warm and cozy home of unconditional acceptance required a ticket, then it wasn't unconditional, was it?

And so, I was trying to resign myself to never getting that unconditional acceptance I yearned for: to feel loved for who I was, flaws and all. And now that my parents were getting up in years, I found myself mostly feeling gratitude for all they had given me. Throughout my life, they had provided for me and cared for me in exemplary ways. They had always been good to support my artistic endeavors and hobbies and my education—anything I was interested in, really. Dad had even gone up to Mound Hill with me and Ben to shoot cemetery statues. That was more than enough. (A couple of years later, Dad would finally say the words I had longed to hear: "I'm proud of you," adding "and your brother, too, of course," which admittedly, diluted the impact.) Still, it was hard to let go of my desire to prove myself.

A trip home to celebrate Dad's eighty-fourth birthday confirmed how potent the push to succeed was in my family and showed how deeply both my brother and I had internalized it.

We were all sitting out on Mom and Dad's closed-in porch, discussing the remarkable career of home girl Nancy Z., daughter of my parents' friends, who had just been hired as the first woman president of a major university in Ohio.

"I wonder how parents get their kids to achieve like that," my brother mused. Believing coercion was necessary, he assumed that it was Nancy's strong-willed mother rather than her mild-mannered father who was behind her success.

He wanted to know how to prod his own daughters. Despite his success as a business man and community leader, he saw himself as deficient as well. I recalled his reaction ten years before to his eldest earning straight A's on her report card: "That's great, but *don't let up!*" Geez. Couldn't he simply praise her success and let her *breathe*? It reminded me of Ray's insight that upper middle-class parents try to spur their kids on by withholding praise and affection.

I thought of my brother's habit of writing people off as "losers" (men, especially) if they hadn't achieved success by his standards.

"It's so wrong to measure a person's worth by their worldly success," I said to Ben on the way home in the car. "I'm so sick of worrying about proving myself to my family."

He replied, "If you don't really agree with their values, then why is living up to them so important?"

Good point. Why, indeed? Because I was conflicted. And maintained a double standard. While I never judged other people on the basis of their success or lack thereof, I continued to judge myself by what I had or hadn't achieved. And then I realized: The person I wanted to prove myself to was myself, but what I most needed was self-acceptance. For the unconditional acceptance I craved, I had been knocking on my own door.

That was when I caught a glimpse of that little girl from the photographs, the "buried child" peeking out of the coffin of forgetting. My four-year-old self whom I had tried to push aside. Accepting *her* was the key to opening the door.

What am I searching for?
What have I forgotten to unbury?

FOR WEEKS, I had been thinking about my childhood and my frustrated ambition, and of course cemeteries and what they had to do with either, but I hadn't thought about that little girl or my vision of her buried. Somehow I'd gotten into my head that my four-year-old self was the flawed one who wore shame on her face and in her slumped, crooked posture; the shy, withdrawn one whom I didn't want to claim as part of me, much less feel empathy toward; the one whose fault it was that I had to prove myself to practically everyone, including my adult self. As much as I wanted to hide from her, she shadowed me, quietly following me wherever I went. Of course, the four-year-old me was just an innocent child—a self-conscious child with low self-esteem to boot. Normally, innocence touched me deeply; it was a quality I cherished. Normally, I would feel empathy for a child who lacked confidence as she did. It puzzled me that I didn't.

A therapist once proclaimed, "Something happened to you!" But *what?* I couldn't think of a single incident that had been traumatic. Yet somehow I had received the message—rightly or wrongly, intentionally or not—that I needed to suppress myself, stay in the background. Although I was constantly monitored and zealously overprotected, probably with the best intentions, I felt unseen. Although I must have talked, I felt unheard. As a child, I was the consummate Good Girl who never did anything worth telling about, while my older brother was the naughty rascal whose shenanigans made for humorous stories retold with relish for decades to come.

Maybe it came down to my being a girl. Maybe it was as simple as that. My parents loved me as their daughter. They had even wanted a girl, my mother had emphasized many times. But there is no getting around the fact that our culture devalues girls and the feminine. The ubiquitous message that females are inferior and deficient and therefore not to be taken seriously was hard to escape. My parents weren't very conscious about that. Perhaps most parents didn't quite know what to do with a little girl; probably many still don't. There must be a conflict between protecting her and granting her the autonomy she needs to grow. Although not a parent, I could understand that.

The deep sadness I had always felt probably came from an awareness of the contempt aimed at women. I thought it also explained why some women (more so than men) were drawn to cemeteries. And I could now see that I had been projecting my repressed grief onto the mournful ladies in stone who graced the cemetery. Was Little Kathy a repository for that grief as well?

Had anything happened to her? Perhaps I would never know. There were probably a thousand gestures, reactions, criticisms and correctives that shaped her and kept her in line. As a sensitive child—too sensitive, I was always told—I would have taken it all to heart. But maybe in the long run, it didn't matter whether I knew or not. Maybe knowing the origin of the wound was less important than healing. I recalled the quote from Jung: "It is what you *are* that heals, not what you *know*."

What was I, then, that would heal me? And what did Little Kathy represent? She was my life force and the part of myself I had lost, my inner child—my soul. She was my creativity, my *voice*. My enthusiasm, my joy. All things I needed to reclaim to heal the wound and become whole.

How could I do that?

I could try active imagination. I could use it to explore my obsession with cemeteries.

I had stumbled onto the Jungian technique, used to access and dialogue with one's own subconscious, soon after I returned from Woodlawn. Active imagination is like a conscious daydream. Once in a receptive state, you let your imagination and subconscious take over and see what comes.

I GO UPSTAIRS to the bedroom, close the blinds to block out the afternoon sun, and stretch out on the bed. I lie there quietly, eyes closed, until I feel relaxed and receptive.

Soon, I find myself in the Mansfield Cemetery, where I had been retaking shots a couple of weeks before. I walk down the entrance road toward the life-sized angel who stands before an enormous cross. But about halfway there, my attention is drawn to a different angel, one I had shot numerous times from various angles. She is a grieving angel, lost in contemplation, her bowed head propped up by fingertips on her forehead and a thumb against her cheek, a melodramatic gesture suggesting a grief too heavy to bear. She is one of my favorites, and I am tempted to go to her, but intuition tells me to continue on.

When I reach the angel who stands before the cross, I feel myself pulled to a tree some yards away. Under the tree, I start digging until I uncover three objects: a white death mask of a woman's face, similar to those of the statues I photograph, eyes closed; a cage with a mouth in it, the lips parted, as if poised to speak; and a large black fountain pen, its tip enclosed with the cap.

I ask the mouth why she's encaged.

"Something happened in your childhood. I can't say what."

Something happened . . . I can't say what?! Part of me wants to know what happened. But part of me doesn't. Regardless, the mouth "can't say" or won't. And where does this leave me anyway? It feels like a dead end. Not quite what I came here for. It encapsulates where I am and where I've been; what I want to do is go beyond that.

I decide to start over.

Again, I am walking down the entrance road of the Mansfield Cemetery toward the angel who stands before the cross. Unlike the grieving angel, this one has a calm demeanor. Her eyes look off into the distance, as though she can see the unseeable. Her commanding stature emanates strength and sure reliability, while her hand on her heart suggests compassion. She is the ideal guide.

When I reach her, I climb up to stand on the ledge in front of her, just as I have done before to get close-ups of her face, which I'd always thought reflected a desire to merge with her. Only this time, I do. I merge with her, become her.

My Angel Self lifts off the pedestal and moves through the air some feet above the path until I come to a nearby tree, which I sense is my destination. When my feet hit the ground, I know I'm supposed to dig here. I kneel on the ground near the tree and start scooping up the earth with my hands.

I move quickly, with urgency. I dig and dig until I unbury a four-year-old little girl, who is also me. She is crying, both from relief that I have come for her at last and from the hurt she has suffered. Her tears break my heart, make me cry, too. I—the one imagining it—feel her pain.

"Why are you crying, Little Girl?" I ask her.

In between sobs, she tries to explain.

"They don't want me—the real me—the excited me. I am too much for them. I have to hide, down myself, bury who I really am . . ."

I gather her into my arms, cradling her, stroke her head, and listen.

"It's okay," I say softly to comfort her. "You are home now."

Epilogue:
God's Playground

HOW WAS IT that, after almost four years of walking in the Village Green, I had never before noticed there was a monument in the park? All this time I thought I had given up walking in cemeteries, but that wasn't exactly the case. Right here, under my nose—in my very own neighborhood—was a place not so very different from Woodlawn.

I made the discovery by chance one summer evening near the end of a walk in the park with Gwennie, the dog Ben and I had adopted after Mandy passed away. A mixed breed with almond-shaped eyes, a long white coat, and very short legs, she resembled a dwarfed Samoyed and was so cute, she drew everyone to her, especially children. She looked like the dog every little girl dreams of having.

As we were walking through the field, Gwennie ran ahead to greet another dog. But when she extended her nose, the other dog snarled and lunged at her.

I rushed to the scene. As I caught up, I recognized the dog's master—a big burly fellow, a little rough looking but, as I recalled, quite pleasant.

"Sorry," I yelled, apologizing for not having Gwen on her leash. "I think we've met before."

"Yes, he's not used to being around other dogs," he said. "Thought I'd take 'im for a walk, while my wife swings our little granddaughter." He gestured toward the small playground across from the pond up ahead.

At the mention of the little girl, his eyes lit up. It was obvious she was his little sweetheart.

We walked on, taking to the outer edge, the grass being rather too high in the center for sandals. I almost took the long way around as usual, but for some reason, I wanted to see that little girl. So we entered the playground, something I'd never done before.

The little granddaughter—a real cutie—turned around in her swing to look at Gwen.

"Hi-i," I sang to her, waving to her with my fingers, the way one does with babies and small children.

She waved back shyly, her eyes glued to Gwen. I continued walking toward the swings.

And then I saw it—first out of the corner of my eye, then on a double take.

Set into the giant rock that the kids like to climb on in the playground was a granite plaque. I moved closer to see what it said.

> THIS PLAYGROUND IS DEDICATED TO
> ALLISON RAE MALARKY
> A BEAUTIFUL SIX YEAR OLD CHILD
> WHO TOUCHED MANY LIVES.
> †
> "YES, ALLISON, THERE ARE SWINGS IN HEAVEN."

A monument. To a child. I was stunned. Few monuments moved me, but this one choked me up. Like so many kids I saw there—that little granddaughter, my neighbors' kids—Allison loved swinging. I could see her, could hear her laughing, squealing with delight as she took to the air in her swing. And I could hear her parents' voices—her mother's especially—answering the precocious child's question, once she grew ill,

"Mommy, are there swings in heaven?" She was not buried there, but remembered in a place she would have loved, a place that captured her innocence and love of life.

Walking back home, I thought of my own un-buried child and the spiritual journey that brought her back to me. It reminded me of medieval mystic Mechthild of Magdeburg's whimsical depiction of God, which she claimed came through her directly from the Divine:

> *I am your playmate. I will lead the child within you*
> *on a wonderful adventure that I have chosen for you.*

And what a fun, wonderful adventure this pilgrimage through the cemetery had been.

Fun? Play? Yes, I know that sounds odd, but as I said in the beginning, I believe the soul works in odd ways. And however odd it sounds, it *had* been fun to walk with Mandy in Woodlawn, to explore Victorian cemeteries and study the symbols I found there, to photograph the beautiful statuary and connect the cemetery to my life and my trials and tribulations in Academe, to reconnect to my spirituality. Of course, a recovering academic's idea of fun, not to mention a taphophile's, might be different from that of other folks.

As I paused before our front door and pulled the key out of my pocket, I felt flush with gratitude. I had always believed this project to be a blessing, and once again, I felt awe that I had been called to undertake it. Before entering the house and crossing the threshold, I gave thanks to the Spirit who had led me on this adventure.

Thank you, dear Friend. Thank you, my most special Playmate.

Acknowledgements

Margaret Atwood is right when she says every writer must make a trip to the underworld alone. But it sure is nice to have people encourage you along the way.

Thanks to the following for their support of this project as I tentatively set foot on the path: Doug Gray and the Columbus Downtown Writers; The Kitchen Table Group—Jeannetta Holliman, Chiquita Mullins Lee, and Barb Thomas, along with other members of the Columbus chapter of the International Women's Writing Guild, Ginger Watkins and Jeanne Marlowe among them; Maureen Murdock and Susan Tiberghien for their feedback at an annual IWWG conference workshop. Thanks to friends who took the time to read individual chapters and celebrate publications: Amy Strawser, Janine Reed, Terry Orr, Jill Gatewood Shaw, Morgan Davies Asbury, Lisa Klein, Veena Kasbekar, and Ariadne sister Susan Glassow. Thanks to Miriam Tamar Levenstein for reading through the manuscript after its completion. Thanks to Carol Christ for her divine encouragement. Thanks to Jane Reeves for starting me on the cemetery path in the first place.

Much appreciation to Marcy Dermansky for helpful suggestions on shaping the manuscript as a whole and to Lynn Houston for giving me the opportunity to publish a lengthy chapter gleaned from the book and her thoughtful suggestions that made it stronger. Eternal gratitude to C. A. Casey and Claudia Wilde of Bedazzled Ink for publishing *Sacred Groves*.

Thanks to Jessica Corey for letting me share her story of the healing garden and to Rick Wager, Superintendent of Woodlawn Cemetery, for information about the uses of the holding vault. Thanks to Deb Wappner Wallace for so generously sharing her expert legal advice.

I want to express deep gratitude to those who helped me find a new home in academia at the Ohio University-Chillicothe Campus: former dean and associate dean, Rich Bebee and Michael Lafreniere; my English

Department colleagues Ron Salomone (who first championed my promotion), Veena Kasbekar, Jan Schmittauer, and Ruth McClain; my art colleagues Margaret McAdams and Dennis Deane, who also offered feedback and encouragement on my photographs. Thanks also to my office mate, Sandy Christman, for her friendship and cemetery photos from her travel outside the country. Teaching my students at OUC was such a pleasure and truly the highlight of my career. Thanks to those from the Twig who wrote strong recommendations for me and to Cheryl Fortman for her continuing friendship and support since teaching there together.

For help with photography and darkroom technique, I want to thank the founders of Insight Studio, Barbara Vogel and the late great John Vaughn, and other members of our collective, including Ron Price, who kept us going for as long as we could before the digital revolution edged us out. Appreciation also to my former husband "Ben" for the use of his Nikon and tips on how to use it. And thanks to Ken Roberts for his permission to use the photograph of his stunning replica of Harold's jaguar hearse; to Don Kessler for sending the photo my way; and to Doyenne of Death, Gail Rubin, for steering me toward Ken and Don.

I want to acknowledge the Association for Gravestone Studies, who provide such a delightful and educational space for us taphophiles, and my taphie friends Beth Santore, Carolyn and Larry Turner, Krista Horrocks, Teresa Straley Lambert, and Kate Hayfield, whose companionship at "cemetery camp" made it all the more fun. I wish I had discovered you sooner.

I also want to acknowledge the Jung community in Saint Louis and here in Central Ohio for giving my story and photographs an audience. Special shout out to Sydney Schardt and Jean Marlowe for their assistance in setting up my solo exhibit and program based on the book.

To my parents, who are no longer living, I owe enormous gratitude for their lifetime support of my professional and creative endeavors and for their generosity, which has made my life so much easier than it might have been. I love them dearly and grieve their loss. I also want to express gratitude to my late brother for the support he gave me. So sorry you didn't live longer, Bro.

And speaking of family, three generations of dogs have given me devoted support throughout my work on this project: Mandy, Gwennie, and now Robby, our little Corgi who has spent many a summer day sitting out back under the red maple tree, amidst the flowers, while I wrote. I think they deserve acknowledgement as much as anyone else.

Finally, utmost gratitude for the two special people to whom this book is dedicated: my former colleague, dear friend and "doula" Deb Nickles, who has read every word of the manuscript as it progressed. Without your constant encouragement, urging me to push and give birth to this book, God knows when I would have finished; and my beloved soulmate and partner, Lynn Slimmer, who came into my life just as I was coming back up from the underworld lavishing me with his love and creative energy, which inspire me in every facet of my life. Thank you, Sweety Pie. I am so blessed to have you both in my life.

Resources

Adler, Gerhardt. *The Living Symbol: A Case Study in the Process of Individualization*. New York: Pantheon, 1961.

Alter, Robert M. and Jane. *The Transformative Power of Crisis: Our Journey to Psychological Healing and Spiritual Awakening*. New York: ReganBooks/HarperCollins, 2000.

Appelbaum, Diana Muir. "Jewish Identity and Egyptian Revival Architecture." *Journal of Jewish Identities* July 2012 5(2), 1-25. Available at https://independent.academic.edu/DianaMuirAppelbaum.

Atwood, Margaret. *Negotiating with the Dead: A Writer on Writing*. Cambridge: Cambridge U, 2002.

Bachelard, Gaston. *The Poetics of Space*. Trans. Maria Jolas. Boston: Beacon, 1969.

Biedermann, Hans. *Dictionary of Symbolism: Cultural Icons and the Meaning Behind Them*. Trans. James Hulbert. New York: Meridian, 1992.

Brady, Emily, and Arto Haapala. "Melancholy as an Aesthetic Emotion." *Contemporary Aesthetics* 1 (2003): http://www.contempaesthetics.org/newvolume/pages/article.php?articleID=214

Brodribb, Somer. *Nothing Mat(t)ers: A Feminist Critique of Postmodernism*. North Melbourne: Spinifex, 1992.

Brown, Frederick. *Pére-Lachaise: Elysium as Real Estate*. New York: Viking, 1973.

A Cemetery Special. Dir. Rick Sebak. PBS, 2005.

Chevalier, Jean, and Alain Gherbrant. *The Penguin Dictionary of Symbols*. 2nd Ed. Trans. John Bachanan-Brown. London: Penguin, 1996.

Chevalier, Tracy. *Falling Angels*. New York: Dutton, 2001.

Christ, Carol P. *Diving Deep and Surfacing: Women Writers on Spiritual Quest*. Boston: Beacon, 1980.

Clark, Sandra Russell. *Elysium, A Gathering of Souls: New Orleans Cemeteries* [Photographs]. Baton Rouge: Louisiana State U, 1997.

Donofrio, Beverly. *Looking for Mary (or, The Blessed Mother & Me)*. New York: Viking Compass, 2000.

Eliot, T. S. *Four Quartets*. San Diego: Harvest/Harcourt Brace, 1943.

Estés, Clarissa Pinkola. *Women Who Run with the Wolves: Mythic Stories of the Wild Woman Archetype*. New York: Ballantine, 1992.

Federico, Annette R., Ed. *Gilbert and Gubar's The Madwoman in the Attic After Thirty Years*. Columbia: U of Missouri, 2011.

Gallop, Jane, Marianne Hirsch, and Nancy K. Miller. "Criticizing Feminist Criticism." *Conflicts in Feminism*. Ed. Marianne Hirsch and Evelyn Fox Keller. New York: Routledge, 1990.

Gilbert, Sandra M., and Susan Gubar. *The Madwoman in the Attic: The Woman Writer and the Nineteenth-Century Literary Imagination*. New Haven: Yale U, 1979.

Grollman, Eric Anthony. "On Racist and Sexist Discrimination in Academia." *Conditionally Accepted: A Space for Scholars on the Margins of Academia, 2 Sept. 2013:* http://conditionally accepted.com/2013/09/02/racism-sexism-academia

Gubar, Susan. *Critical Condition: Feminism at the Turn of the Century*. New York: Columbia U, 2000.

_____. *Rooms of Our Own*. Urbana: U of Illinois, 2006.

_____. "What Ails Feminist Criticism? *Critical Inquiry* (Summer 1998), available on line.

Hillman, James. *Blue Fire: Selected Writings by James Hillman*. Ed. Thomas Moore. New York: Harper Perennial, 1989.

Hobbs, June Hadden. "Elizabeth Stuart Phelps and the Gates Ajar on Tombstones Then and Now." Unpublished paper delivered at the Association for Gravestone Studies Conference, Granville, Ohio, 2009.

_____. "Tombstone Erotics and Gender in the Graveyards of the South," *Southern* Quarterly 39.3 (Spring 2001), 11.

Horne, Ronald William. *Forgotten Faces: A Window into Our Immigrant Past*. San Francisco: Personal Genesis, 2004.

Jack, Dana. *Silencing the Self: Women and Depression*. Cambridge: Harvard U, 1991.

Jaschik, Scott. "'Quiet Desperation' of Academic Women." *Inside Higher Ed.* 12 June 2008: https://www.insidehighered.com

Johnson, Robert A. (with Jerry M. Ruhl). *Balancing Heaven and Earth: A Memoir of Visions, Dreams, and Realizations*. San Francisco: HarperSanFrancisco, 1998.

_____. *Inner Work: Using Dreams and Active Imagination for Personal Growth.* San Francisco: Harper & Row, 1986.

_____. *Owning Your Own Shadow: Understanding the Dark Side of the Psyche.* San Francisco: HarperSanFrancisco, 1994.

Keister, Douglas. *Stories in Stone: A Field Guide to Cemetery Symbolism and Iconography.* Salt Lake City: Gibbs Smith, 2004.

Kelsey, Karen. *The Professor Is In.* Blog. http://theprofessorisin.com.

Kessler, Carol Farley. "*The Gates Ajar.*" In *American History through Literature, 1870-1920* [Electronic Resource]. Ed. Janet Gabler-Hover and Robert Sattelmeyer. Farmington Hills, MI: Gale, 2006. Also available on line at http://www.enotes.com/gates-ajar-reference/gates-ajar

Kidd, Sue Monk. *The Dance of the Dissident Daughter: A Woman's Journey from Christian Tradition to the Sacred Feminine.* San Francisco: HarperSanFrancisco, 1996.

Laughlin, Clarence John. *The Personal Eye.* Exhibition Catalogue [Photographs]. New York: Aperture, 1973.

Lehrer, Jonah. "Feeling Sad Makes Us More Creative." *Wired,* 19 Oct. 2010: http://www.wired.com/2010/10/feeling-sad-makes-us-more-creative/

Lifton, Jay. *The Protean Self: Human Resilience in the Age of Fragmentation.* New York: BasicBooks, 1993.

Linden-Ward, Blanche. "Strange but Genteel Pleasure Grounds: Tourist and Leisure Uses of Nineteenth-Century Rural Cemeteries." In *Cemeteries and Gravemarkers.* Ed. Richard E. Meyer. Logan UT: Utah State U, 1992.

Livingston, James C. *Anatomy of the Sacred: An Introduction to Religion.* 5th Ed. Upper Saddle River, NJ: Pearson/Prentice Hall, 2005.

Lynch, Thomas. *Bodies in Motion and at Rest: On Metaphor and Mortality.* New York: W. W. Norton, 2000.

_____. *The Undertaking: Life Studies from the Dismal Trade.* New York: Penguin, 1997.

Mann, Sally. *What Remains* [Includes Photographs]. Boston: Bullfinch, 2003. Also made into a 2008 DVD.

Martin, Jane Roland. *Coming of Age in Academe: Rekindling Women's Hopes and Reforming the Academy.* New York: Routledge UP, 2000.

Martin, Linette. *Sacred Doorways: A Beginner's Guide to Icons,* Brewster, MA: Paraclete, 2002.

Modleski Tania. *Feminism without Women: Culture and Criticism in a "Postfeminist"Age.* New York: Routledge, 1991.

Moi, Toril. *Sexual/Textual Politics: Feminist Literary Theory.* London: Methune, 1985.

Moore, Thomas. *Dark Nights of the Soul: A Guide to Finding Your Way through Life's Ordeals.* New York: Gotham/Penguin, 2004.

_____. *Original Self: Living with Paradox and Originality.* New York: HarperCollins, 2000.

Murdock, Maureen. *The Heroine's Journey: Women's Quest for Wholeness.* Boston: Shambala, 1990.

Niffenegger, Audrey. *Fearful Symmetry.* New York: Scribner, 2009.

Nuxhall, Phil. *Beauty in the Grove: Spring Grove Cemetery & Arboretum* [Includes Photographs]. Wilmington, OH: Orange Frazer, 2009.

O'Driscoll, Dennis. "Someone." In *Inventions of Farewell: A Book of Elegies.* Ed. Sandra M. Gilbert. New York: Norton, 2001.

O'Grady, John P. *Grave Goods: Essays of a Peculiar Nature.* Salt Lake City: U of Utah, 2001.

Otto, Rudolph. *The Idea of the Holy.* Trans. John W. Harvey. London: Oxford U, 1958.

Phelps, Elizabeth Stuart. *The Gate Ajar.* 1868. Ed. Helen Sootin Smith. Cambridge, MA: Belknap Press of Harvard U, 1964.

Powers-Douglas, Minda. *Cemetery Walk: Journey into the Art, History, and Society of the Cemetery and Beyond.* AuthorHouse, 2005.

Reis, Patricia. *Through the Goddess: A Woman's Way of Healing.* New York: Continuum, 1991.

_____. *Daughters of Saturn: From Father's Daughter to Creative Woman.* New York: Continuum, 1995.

Rilke, Rainer Maria. *Sonnets to Orpheus.* Trans. M. D. Herter Norton. New York: W. W. Norton, 1942.

Robinson, David. *Beautiful Death: Art of the Cemetery* [Photographs]. New York: Viking Penguin, 1996.

_____. *Saving Graces* [Photographs]. New York: Norton, 1995.

Sheehy, Gail. *Passages: Predictable Crises of Adult Life.* New York: Dutton, 1976.

Shlain, Leonard. *The Alphabet Versus the Goddess: The Conflict Between Word and Image.* New York: Viking, 1998.

Sloane, David Charles. *The Last Great Necessity: Cemeteries in American History (Creating the North American Landscape).* Baltimore: The Johns Hopkins U, 1995.

Smith, Jeffery. *Where the Roots Reach for Water: A Personal and Natural History of Melancholia.* New York: North Point/Farrar, Straus and Giroux, 1999.

Stevens, Amanda. *The Restorer.* MIRA: Toronto, 2011.

_____. *The Kingdom.* MIRA: Toronto, 2012.

_____. *The Prophet.* MIRA: Toronto, 2012.

_____. *The Visitor.* MIRA: Toronto, 2016.

_____. *The Sinner.* MIRA: Toronto, 2016.

_____. *The Awakening.* MIRA: Toronto, 2017.

Taxel, Barney. *The Lake View Cemetery: Photographs from Cleveland's Historic Landmark.* Akron: Ringtaw, 2014.

Taylor, Sarah Stewart. *Judgment of the Grave.* New York: St. Martin's/Minotaur, 2005.

_____. *Mansions of the Dead.* New York: St. Martin's/Minotaur, 2004.

_____. *O' Artful Death.* New York: St. Martin's/Minotaur, 2003.

_____. *Still as Death.* New York: St. Martin's/Minotaur, 2006.

Todd, Janet. *Feminist Literary History.* New York: Routledge, 1988.

"The Undertaking." *Frontline.* PBS Documentary on Thomas Lynch. Dir. Miri Navasky and Karen O'Connor, 2007. Available on line at http://www.pbs.org/wgbh/frontline/film/ undertaking.

Vogler, Christopher. *The Writer's Journey: Mythic Structure for Writers.* 2nd Ed. Studio City, CA: Michael Wiese Productions, 1998.

Weaver, Helen. *The Daisy Sutra: Conversations with My Dog.* Woodstock, NY: Buddha Rock, 2001.

Williams, Terry Tempest. *Leap.* New York: Pantheon, 2000.

Woolf, Virginia. "Professions for Women." In *Death of the Moth and Other Essays.* New York: Harcourt Brace Javonovich, 1974.

The Young and the Dead. HBO documentary about Tyler Cassity's restoration of Hollywood Memorial Cemetery. Dir. Robert Pulcini and Shari Springer Berman, 2003.

Notes

1. Data from the Association of American University Professors, as reported in Gloria Steinem's foreword to Jane Roland Martin's *Coming of Age in Academe: Rekindling Women's Hopes and Reforming the Academy*.

2. In her 2014 "The Status of Women in Academia," Rachel Croson reports that "Women are less likely to be granted tenure in every field." For a specific example, Eric Anthony Grollman quoted a study of tenure rates at the University of Southern California in his 2013 article, "On Racist and Sexist Discrimination in Academia": "Since 1998, 92% of white males who were considered for tenure got it. During the same period of time only 55% percent of women and minority candidates were granted tenure." Scott Jaschik's 2008 *Inside Higher Ed* article, "'Quiet Desperation' of Academic Women," chronicles the deep frustration women in academia experience due to discriminatory practices and values. Suggesting that survival tips are still very much necessary, in her recent blog, *The Professor Is In*, former professor Karen Kelsky offers advice to women who aspire to succeed in academic settings, along with support for those who wish to leave academia as she did. All of these sources are available on line.

3. Hans Biedermann, *Dictionary of Symbolism* 188.

4. Thanks to June Hadden Hobbs for sparking my interest in Phelps. See also Carol Farley Kessler.

5. Qtd. in Blanche Linden-Ward 300.

6. The 2011 edition includes entries on notable African Americans, which is especially important in a town with a sizeable African-American population, and champions of other causes such as women's suffrage. The fact that women are featured in their own right is a change from the first edition.

7. Qtd. in David Charles Sloane, *The Last Great Necessity* 55-56. For the history of the Victorian Garden Cemetery, I rely heavily on this seminal study.

8. In the old graveyards of some mental hospitals, patients' gravestones are marked with numbers only, others include *M* or *F* for gender.

9. Toril Moi, *Sexual/Textual Politics*, quoting Barthes' "The Death of the Author" 63.

10. Mary Jacobus, qtd.in Janet Todd, *Feminist Literary History* 76.

11. See Gilbert and Gubar's T*he Madwoman in the Attic After Thirty Years*, Ed. Annette R. Federico (2011), and *Gubar's Critical Condition* (from which the quote was taken) and *Rooms of Our Own*.

12. Quote from Shakespeare's *King Lear*.

13. When his disciples saw the transfigured Jesus on Mt. Tabor, "His face shone like the sun and His clothes became as white as the light" *Matthew 17:3*.

14. From Sylvia Plath's *The Bell Jar.*

15. Leonard Shlain, *The Alphabet Versus the Goddess* 432.

16. The phrase "exile in guyville" is Liz Phair's.

17. From Dennis O'Driscoll's "Someone."

18. From *The Cemetery Special.* Cypress Lawn is in Colma, California.

19. All Niffenegger quotes are from "Audrey Niffenegger: This Much I Knew," *The Guardian* 4 May 2013, available on line.

20. See Chevalier's website on *Falling Angels.*

21. Patricia Reis, *Through the Goddess* 210.

22. Maureen Murdock, *The Heroine's Journey* 105, 88. Murdock's reconstruction was inspired by a conversation she'd had with Campbell. When she asked him about a female hero's journey, he said there wasn't one; she was the object of the hero's quest.

Kathleen Davies earned her Ph.D. from Indiana University and taught English and Women's & Gender Studies for many years before retiring to write full time. Her creative nonfiction has appeared in *Imitation Fruit, Ray's Road Review*, and *South Loop Review*, among other publications. She lives in Columbus, Ohio with her husband, Lynn, and their incorrigible Welsh Corgi, Robby. Visit Kathleen at www.kathleendaviesauthors.com.